UNIONS AND THE LAW

Unions and the Law

CAMPBELL BALFOUR

*Department of Industrial
Relations,
University College, Cardiff*

SAXON Ⓢ HOUSE | LEXINGTON BOOKS

Published by

SAXON HOUSE, D. C. Heath Ltd.
Westmead, Farnborough, Hants, England

Jointly with

LEXINGTON BOOKS, D. C. Heath & Co.
Lexington, Mass. U.S.A.

ISBN 0 347 010032
LC No. 73–5248

Printed in The Netherlands by D. Reidel Book Manufactures, Dordrecht

Contents

Preface

This is not a text book on labour law, but an account of the contemporary crisis in industrial relations. It is also an attempt to look at the place of law in labour relations, and to remind ourselves that making law is one process, while enforcing it is another. A comprehensive law, such as the Industrial Relations Act 1971, cannot be separated from its political and social context, and I have tried to explain this.

There are difficulties in writing about a process that is still unfolding. But the IR Act raises the whole question of social control and the democratic consensus on which law must be based. The web of the law stretches from the House of Lords to the pickets on London Docks, and its strength is mainly in the mind of the citizen. Law which is widely ignored or flouted ceases to be law.

I have acknowledged my reliance on many writers, books, pamphlets, articles and newspapers throughout this work, though my interpretation of their writings reflects my own views as well as my mistakes. I should include in the previous statement the many discussions I have had, ranging over the whole theme of law and labour relations, with my colleagues, Professor George Thomason and Mr Peter Anthony.

CAMPBELL BALFOUR
University College,
Cardiff

March 1973

Introduction

The origin of this book took shape when I worked on a study of incomes policy (*Incomes Policy and the Public Sector*, Routledge & Kegan Paul, London 1972). It became clear that a combination of inflationary pressure in the economy and the passing of the Industrial Relations Act 1971, had resulted in a sharp reaction by the trade unions, and a worsening of industrial strife as unions and groups of workers used industrial power to press their claims and resist or ignore the legislation designed to curb them.

Newspapers argued throughout 1972 and early 1973 that the conflict between Government and unions had reached a crisis point. Concern, real or imagined, over trade union activities, was at its highest point since the General Strike of 1926, and the number of working days lost (24 million in 1972) was the greatest since 1926. The concern was due to the realisation that modern British industry was more complex, highly capitalised and interdependent than ever before. Numbers of unions or workers could cause large scale discomfort and disruption through strikes or industrial action in coal, gas, electricity, refuse disposal, docks, rail and air, while those in the car, newspaper, building and other industries acted as frontrunners for other workers in their wage claims. These confrontations are caused by, and are a response to, the rapid inflation of the late 1960s and early 1970s.

While most public and legal attention has been focused on the Industrial Relations Act 1971 and its effects on industrial relations, many politicians and lawyers appear to have ignored the legal aspects of wage control. The attempts at government regulation of wages and wage levels, with periodic attempts at statutory enforcement, bring wages into the realm of law in the same way that the behaviour of motorists is a matter of public concern and regulation. The well loved trilogy of full employment, stable prices and free collective bargaining, seen as a rosy promise at each General Election, have each been questioned in turn. Full employment has come to mean up to one million unemployed, while stable prices now need an 'escalator clause' in wage agreements to make them possible. The last of the trio, free collective bargaining, came under fire in the incomes policy of the 1964–1970 Labour Government. The 1970 Conservative Government, after being elected on a promise to cherish and uphold free collective bargaining, saw by 1972 that the British economy might not survive without third party Government intervention on the level of wage settlements as a substitute for the failure of the Industrial Relations Act. The rule of law promised in industrial relations in 1970 failed to prevent strikes or make unions responsible for

1

them. Wage and price inflation led to the 'back-up' of statutory control, which in turn brings the question of how to enforce such laws in industrial relations.

The combination of legal enforcement against unauthorised wage increases and unofficial strike action designed to further wage increases, is not usually found in the legal texts. Lawyers have taken action for workers' wages against Government attempts to limit them (see the action of the Association of Scientific Technical and Managerial Staffs (ASTMS) in September 1966), but they deal with this as a breach of contract by the employer. The traditional right of the employer to sack men has also been curtailed by the 1971 Act.

The question of law and labour relations, seen from the view of the practitioner in industrial relations, may be as useful as the view of the lawyer. I wrote in *Incomes Policy* that the period 1965–1970 represented a change in government thinking about incomes policy from the advice of the economist to the advice of the lawyer. As industrial relations occupies a disputed area between law, economics, politics and sociology, I propose to examine law and labour relations from that vantage point. When MPs in opposition can advocate supporting some laws and opposing others which they claim to be 'politically motivated' the traditional respect for the law needs examination. When a sociologist can quote the following comment on breaches of collective agreements

> It is easy for employers to talk about the 'sanctity of contracts', because they are seldom under any inducement to break them. But the workmen have sometimes to choose between breaking their contracts and breaking faith with their fellow-workers, in such a way as to allow the employer to worsen the conditions of employment. Under such conditions, workmen cannot be expected to keep their contracts; indeed, they would be wrong to do so, if it is in their power to resist. (G. D. H. Cole, 'British Trade Unions Today', London 1939, in R. Hyman *Strikes*, Fontana, London 1972, p. 38)

he poses sharply the whole question as to whether trade union 'militants' will regard a contract as influencing their conduct in any way. This point of view is far from academic: the TUC voted 'not to co-operate with the Industrial Relations Act' while some unions went further and refused to appear before a court of law (the National Industrial Relations Court) when summoned to do so. This is contempt of court, and large fines may be levied on unions. When the Government spokesman said that trade unions should obey the law, some Opposition MPs voiced their support for defiance of the court by unions. Under these tensions, a confrontation between some

2

unions and the law of the country is possible. The drama has been heightened in the early months of 1973 by the wage-price 'freeze' begun on 6 November 1972. Worsening economic conditions, increasing industrial unrest, or continuing inflation could lead to a 1973 General Election with the rallying cry 'Who runs the nation? Government or unions?' What begins as a question about law in labour relations becomes a question about power in society. But we take as our starting point the question asked by the Donovan Report: 'What can the law do to help improve our industrial relations?'.

This book sets out to describe and analyse the role of law in industrial relations, and to explain why the Industrial Relations Act 1971 became a dead, or enfeebled, albatross round the neck of Mr Heath, instead of a phoenix rising from the ashes of industrial strife. It is not a book about labour law, of which there is an abundance, or about the Industrial Relations Act, about which there are several. This is an attempt to bridge the gap between the lawyer and the trade union official, not by explaining one to the other so that the lion and the lamb lie down together, but by looking closely at the attempts over the years, though chiefly between 1969 and 1973, to introduce law into industrial relations.

Labour law is made by lawyers and politicians, mainly for lawyers, but it is about the activities and hopes of millions of workers, many organised in trade unions. The resulting legal judgements are often sterile, the classic example being the judgement of the House of Lords on the picketing activities of London dockers. This book is essentially a non-legal look at law in industrial relations. Just as war is too serious to be left to the generals, law is too important to be left to the lawyers. As we shall see later, Parliament sometimes takes a different view of what labour law should be, especially on major issues, from that of the courts.

Numbers of books have been written on labour law but they have been mainly concerned with what the law says or what Parliament has decreed. Valuable though this is, it fails to notice the distinction between what the law says and what the law does. We can illustrate this by looking at the law relating to motorists: there is a speed limit of 30 mph in towns and 70 mph on motorways, yet the speeding motorist has as much chance of being prosecuted as he has of winning a football pool; there is a law against drunken driving, yet every night some half million drive while drunk, while the numbers prosecuted yearly are only a few thousand. In spite of this dichotomy between what the law says and what it does, Cabinet Ministers can still tell approving crowds, in relation to industrial disputes, that workers cannot choose which laws to obey and which to defy. Law, like peace, is indivisible, and widespread evasion of the law in some areas makes it easier to ignore in others.

Law, in the last analysis, rests on the consent of the governed. This makes possible the enforcement of law against the minority who break the law. Yet one of the paradoxes of law relating to trade unions is that law usually relates to individuals, while unions or strikers act in groups.

When large numbers break the law, the law is virtually unenforceable. Law, as the Lord Chancellor said in 1972, is a 'gigantic confidence trick' underlining the helplessness of law enforcement agencies if respect for the law disappears. This helplessness was demonstrated in the classic case of the Kent miners in 1941. Strikes were forbidden, we were fighting daily against German invasion threats, yet the Kent miners struck. The Government decided to act, but had to conduct a farcical operation. Strike leaders agreed to plead guilty, but thousands of miners stopped work during the trial and the few days during which the leaders were in jail. The Government had to release them so that coal would be mined. Thirty-one years later, the same situation occurred in the London docks when five dockers were imprisoned.

Today the situation is worse in some ways than in 1941. We are not at war, yet the mood of 1972–73 is more truculent and militant than it has been for fifty years. While large-scale violence is unknown in this country, picketing in 1972 was more violent than at any time since 1926.

Do we need a legal framework for industrial relations?

The Conservative Government of 1970 said that it was needed, and the country's view, measured by opinion pols and election themes, seemed to coincide. Yet few people asked the question 'why now?'. Why was it necessary to have a legal framework for industrial relations, when industry had functioned for the greater part of the twentieth century without such legislation? Professor Kahn-Freund, in his book *Labour and the Law* (1972), points out that the role of the labour lawyer is less important than some others, including the 'practical economist'. He adds 'I regard law as a secondary force in human affairs, and especially in labour relations' (Kahn-Freund, *op. cit.*, p. 3). When so distinguished a labour lawyer makes such a confession, one wonders why the government decided to introduce the 1971 labour legislation. The answer, or its beginnings, may be found in Kahn-Freund's view that the 'reasonably well functioning of labour relations is one of the great achievements of British civilisation. This system of collective bargaining rests on a balance of the collective forces of management and organised labour' (Kahn-Freund, *op. cit.*, p. 1). We must then believe that, by 1970, this collective balance had broken down or had been heavily weighted on the side of labour.

Previous changes in the twentieth century had been made by a Conservative

4

government in 1901, and a Liberal one in 1909, only to be reversed after trade union and political pressure. On each occasion when the wave of strikes rose to a peak, counter measures were taken: the Taff Vale Act in 1901, the Trade Disputes Act in 1927. The wave of militancy between 1911 and 1913 was effectively stopped by the First World War. Apart from legislation and the accident of war, labour was kept in check by unemployment.

Full employment after 1945 did not lead to major strikes for some twenty years. Employers paid higher wages and raised prices, and inflation alternated between 'demand-pull', based on spending power and shortage of goods, and 'cost-push', based on the rise of factor prices on the supply side, chiefly the cost of labour.

Full employment and the consequent inflation may have been among the main factors in the rising strike rate of the 1960s, but strikes were at a relatively level rate with less than 4 million man-days lost per year until 1967. Since then the man-days lost have risen dramatically between 1968 and 1972 from 4,719,000 to 24 million.

The main argument of this book will be that successive governments were content to leave industrial relations to the balance of union and employer interests, until it appeared that 'cost-push' inflation based on wage increases was the major cause of inflation. Once this view had been accepted, the Government view (even that of a Labour Government) was that laws should be passed which would make the unofficial strike, against the advice of union leaders, far less frequent. The Labour Government gave up their attempt in the face of strong trade union and back-bench MP pressure, on the grounds that the TUC had given 'a solemn binding promise' to use their best efforts to intervene in unofficial disputes. In spite of this, the strike rate mounted to 10,908,000 in 1970. The rising strike rate continued through 1971-72, in spite of the comprehensive Industrial Relations Act of the Conservatives in 1971, though one result was the decline in the number of unofficial strikes, and the increase in the number of large official strikes.

Can laws be enforced in industrial relations?

This question lies at the heart of the matter, like the earwig in the rose. A Conservative government stands in the public eye for 'law and order' and makes this a plank in their election platform. The Industrial Relations Act was, according to opinion polls, welcomed by the public. After the Act was passed and strikes grew in size and damaging effect, voices were raised asking for the law to be involved. Not, however, the voices of the larger companies, who quietly ignored the Act. Some of the smaller companies invoked the

Act and, after some court cases and national strikes, the Conservative Government virtually retreated from the industrial battlefield of its own choosing. The trade unions had opted for 'non-compliance' with the Act and had refused to register. The jailing of five dockers led to a national dock strike and the men were released. During this, and other strikes, violent scenes took place as pickets clashed with police and with other workers who disagreed with the strike. By October 1972 the Government appeared to be ignoring the Act, and some of the small employers who had originally gone to the National Industrial Relations Court (NIRC) for justice under the law, decided to abandon the legal approach and reach results through collective negotiations.

The Conservative retreat was not announced publicly. Mr Carr, the pilot of the Act through Parliament, answered the criticisms of inactivity over violent picketing by telling the 1972 Conservative Conference 'let me make it clear, obstruction and intimidation are absolutely contrary to the law'. The law of picketing being clear, the police should enforce it. The difficulty begins here, as the law cannot be enforced against large numbers who break it. The other difficulty, as in the docks, was that the arrest of pickets by the police, and their imprisonment, could begin a national strike in some vital industry, or prolong an existing strike.

A further difficulty for the Government was, after two and a half years of confrontation, that inflation was continuing at a rapid rate. By October 1972 discussions on a voluntary incomes and prices policy had taken place between the Government, employers and unions. As one *quid pro quo* for any co-operation, the unions asked that the Industrial Relations Act be 'put on ice'. The talks failed, and the Government brought in a statutory pay standstill for ninety days, followed by a 'Phase II pay policy', restricting pay and price rises. Legislation to control unions had proved ineffective, so the legislation shifted to wages. The results lie in the future, but this account of the attempts to regulate trade unions might help future policy makers. My hope is that they will remember the words of Mr Justice Holmes many years ago: 'The life of the law is not logic, but experience'.

1 Law and the Unions

The foundation of British trade union law for one hundred years was the Act of 1871, buttressed by the Act of 1875. This endured, with some set-backs, until the Industrial Relations Act of 1971, which changed the legal basis of industrial relations from 'voluntarism' to 'legalism'. To quote the words of the Conservative Election Manifesto of 1970, it was 'to provide a legal framework for industrial relations and thus reduce industrial conflict'.

Public irritation against trade unions was expressed in 1867 in much the same words ('a number of unscrupulous men') as were used in 1967. But the explosion of gunpowder in a 'blackleg's' house in Sheffield led to public demands for an inquiry into union activities and a Royal Commission was set up. The unions co-operated with the Commission as a court decision of 1867 had declared that a union was 'in restraint of trade' and 'an illegal association'. The case arose out of the action of the Boilermakers Society against a local treasurer for having wrongful possession of £24. The judges found against the union, and the unions found, to their dismay, that they could not legally protect their funds. The unions massed their forces, and deployed their representation so that the Royal Commission would see that the leaders were responsible men and not agitators. The Webbs write that the unions portrayed themselves in the role of insurance companies rather than strike leaders, whereas the employers still insisted on the individual bargain with an employee and objected to the principle of trade unionism (S. and B. Webb *History of Trade Unionism*, 1919 edition, p. 266).

The Royal Commission did not give unions the 'right to strike' as the post Second World War constitutions of France, Germany and Italy did, but they conceded that unions should not be prosecuted. For example,

> no act should be illegal of committed by a workman unless it was equally illegal if committed by any other person; and secondly, that no act by a combination of men should be regarded as criminal if it would not have been criminal in a single person (Webb, *op. cit.*, p. 270).

The unions regarded this finding, and the Act of 1871, as a partial triumph. The Act was linked with the Criminal Law Amendment Act, which severely limited the activities of pickets as 'molestation' and 'intimidation'. The next stage of the struggle to lift the burden of the Criminal Law Amendment Act ended in 1875, when the Government made peaceful picketing legal and collective bargaining thereby more effective. These changes in labour law were related to the growing electoral power of the newly enfranchised worker and to the growing membership of trade unions, whose numbers doubled between 1871 and 1875. In a sense, parliamentary legislation followed the electoral returns as surely as trade followed the flag.

The union argument was based on the reciprocal right to withdraw labour against the employer's right to hire and fire:

> We reserve to ourselves the right to work for, or to refuse to work for, an employer according to the circumstances of the case, just as the master has the right to discharge a workman, or workmen (Webb, *op. cit.*, p. 295).

This remained the fulcrum of the union case for many years, although in the 1950s and 1960s the question of 'job property rights' and the demand for employers to treat their workers as 'social capital' circumscribed the employer's right to dismiss without hindrance.

Soon after their new found freedom from prosecution the unions ran into greater employer resistance during the 'Great Depression' and their numbers fell rapidly in such unions as the Agricultural Workers. The revival of union membership in the 1880s came through the development of the general unions who enrolled the semi and unskilled workers. This led to an increasing political militancy at the TUC gatherings and more militant industrial policies were put forward. Outside the union movement the various 'isms, liberalism, socialism, communism, anarchism, methodism and other religious groups who preached the 'social gospel', were spreading their ideas of the better society and were listened to by many, who in turn filtered the new radicalism through factory discussions and neighbourhood proselytising.

In spite of the advances in legal freedom, the unions ran into a number of conflicting judgements in which the courts exercised their power in interpreting the intentions of Parliament. One of those was Allen *v.* Flood (1898) where two shipyard carpenters were engaged in a demarcation dispute with the secretary of the local branch of the Boilermakers' Society. The men had served an apprenticeship in which they were taught to do wood and iron work on ships, and on the disputed job they had been doing iron work. The Boilermakers' secretary, Allen, objected to this, and threatened to withdraw his men if Flood and Taylor were not discharged from the job. The House of Lords decided that the Boilermakers were not acting illegally in refusing to work with the shipwrights.

This decision for the unions had been influenced by the case of Mogul S. S. Co. *v.* McGregor, Gow and Co. (1892) where the courts upheld the right of business groups to band against competitors. On the principle of legal equilibrium, trade unions were thought to have the same right.

A decision which went against the unions was that of Lyons *v.* Wilkins (1896), in which Lyons, a leather-goods manufacturer, had his premises picketed by a small union of leather workers, of whom Wilkins was the secretary. He obtained an injunction against the pickets, even though no violence or intimidation was practised. The union appealed against the injunction, but lost in the courts. This verdict worried the trade unions considerably as they had been sure that Parliament had intended to legalise peaceful picketing. However, public opinion outside Parliament had been influenced by the pressure of employers associations who were vociferous on the rights of individual workers to work where they pleased. To assist them in this aim, and to make strikes less effective, a man called William Collison set up the National Free Labour Association in 1893. His intention was mainly to supply labour to employers who were strike bound. To break the strike his men had to cross picket lines and this had been difficult in some areas, although his greatest successes had been in cosmopolitan areas such as docks and shipping.

The next landmark in labour law was the Taff Vale judgement of 1901, which placed the existence of the unions once more in legal jeopardy. In mid 1900 there was a strike on the Taff Vale railway in South Wales and the company claimed an injury. They brought a civil suit for damages against the Amalgamated Society of Railway Servants (ASRS). The importance of the judgement was that action was taken against the union by the employers, and not against individual workers. This established the principle that a trade union could be sued as a collectivity, and its funds made liable for any tortious act, whether committed by its officials or by members who were acting as agents. The importance of the judgement is the similarity between this decision and those made in 1972 by the National Industrial Relations Court (NIRC), whose judgement was reversed by the Court of Appeal, and upheld by the House of Lords in a few short months in 1972. Beasley, general manager of the Taff Vale Railway, took out an injunction against the ASRS. The strike was settled after some days but the case continued, with the Society winning in the Court of Appeal and losing in the House of Lords. As the Lord Chancellor put it:

> If the legislature has created a thing which can own property, which can employ servants, which can inflict injury, it must be taken, I think, to have impliedly given the power to make it sueable in a court of law for injuries purposely done by its authority and procurement (House of Lords, 22 July 1901).

This was the principle accepted by the Law Lords, and the ASRS were liable for damages and costs, about £30,000. (A railway trade union official of the time told the writer that Beasley framed the cheque and hung it behind his desk. When strikes were threatened he (Beasley) used to point to the cheque and say 'That's what happened to you last time'.)

The decision placed the unions under a grave legal threat to their funds, as a strike might render them liable for damages to the point of bankruptcy. Their energies were now funnelled into the political field and they began to support the young Labour Party in rapidly increasing numbers, as well as putting pressure on the Liberal opposition to promise to introduce a new Act repealing the Taff Vale judgement. The sweeping Liberal victory of 1906, with Labour support, brought legal immunity for the unions acting as unions. The decision has been called a 'negative statute', as it gave immunity to peaceful picketing in a dispute, as well as from economic torts. The success of their political campaign confirmed the unions in their aversion to the law courts. Parliament, they noted, had reaffirmed their rights to strike and picket, whereas the courts seemed to deny them these rights (the word 'rights' means freedom from prosecution, as British unions do not have constitutional 'rights' going by the Continental definition). In an important sense, the £30,000 lost by the ASRS could be viewed as an investment which paid a political dividend.

But the law had its political arm in the House of Lords and their opportunity came in 1909 when Walter Osborne, Secretary of the Walthamstow branch of the ASRS, took his union to court on the grounds that they should not raise political levies to support the Labour candidates for Parliament. Osborne himself was a Liberal, who held the view that unions were a 'purely industrial organisation'. He had campaigned against the ASRS affiliation to the fledgling Labour Party, then the Labour Representation Committee. Losing his case in the Chancery Court, Osborne moved on to the Court of Appeal, where 'judges readily grasped the importance of the issues', putting their views in the guise of questions and statements from the Bench. For example,

> Lord Justice Farwell: I thought there was some element of freedom left in this country; but that may be the result enforced by starvation – that is to say, by turning him out of his Trade Union or out of his employment (W. V. Osborne *My Case*, Eveleigh Nash, London 1910, p. 31).

Lord Justice Farwell was thus able, after nine years, to renew his legal judgements on the activities of the ASRS. As Mr Justice Farwell, he was the judge in the Taff Vale case of 1901, whose adverse judgement on the union was reversed by the Court of Appeal and later vindicated by the House of Lords.

Once again the House of Lords' views on trade union activities were reversed by the House of Commons. The Liberal government brought in a salary for MPs in 1911, and in 1913 unions were allowed to 'contract out' of such a levy, which was held in a separate fund to other union funds. The membership had to be balloted on the political levy.

During the years between the Osborne judgement of 1909 and the Trade Union Act of 1913, which helped restore the union political fighting funds, there were many outbreaks of industrial unrest and some lengthy strikes. The most famous was the Cambrian strike in South Wales, which resulted in the Tonypandy riots of 1911, around which the legend grew that Winston Churchill had sent troops to quell the Tonypandy miners. Contemporary accounts certainly suggest that South Wales was like an immense army camp, with a number of regiments and groups of policemen billeted at different points. There was also the seamen's strike which spread to a number of large ports. Much of the ideology behind the strikes led to the syndicalists, who were contemptuous of social change through Parliament and wanted to seize power through industrial action. 'The Miners' Next Step' was the most famous pamphlet of the movement, advocating nationalisation and workers' control. Later variants in workers' control were the Guild Socialism ideas of some journalists and intellectuals, who wished to attain power by democratic means.

It has been argued that the influence of the syndicalists and revolutionary socialists has been greatly exaggerated, partly by the Press and Parliament. The Labour Party before 1914 was still a minority party, and South Wales, now almost solid Labour, was then a Liberal stronghold. Some of the industrial discontent could be traced to rising prices between 1909 and 1913. There was great concern in those years, as there is now in the 1970s, over the wave of strikes. Observers pointed out that the old docile worker who haggled over a shilling here and there had gone, and was being replaced by men who saw the strikes as a weapon to change capitalist society. H. G. Wells wrote that 'the new fashioned strike is far less of a haggle, far more a display of temper'. Wells saw the problems of industry being solved by industry and added 'leave labour to the lawyers, and we shall go very deeply into trouble indeed before this business is over' (H. G. Wells *The Labour Unrest, Daily Mail* pamphlet, London, May 1912, p. 10).

Henry Pelling writes of the growth in conciliation and arbitration boards as a substitute for legal action, from 'sixty-four in 1894 to 162 in 1905 and 325 in 1913'. This was in line with radical feeling about the expensive and time wasting procedures of the law and the plea for 'arbitration before litigation' was frequently made. Pelling mentions the union leaders' 'complete distrust of the judiciary, which they believed to be ignorant of industrial problems and animated by upper class prejudices against unionism' (H. Pelling *A History of British Trade Unionism*, Pelican, London 1963, p. 143).

One of the classic tests of government law and trade union defiance came in the First World War. Under the Munitions of War Act the trade unions found themselves restricted in a number of ways, the chief one being the virtual banning of the strike and the introduction of compulsory arbitration. But a large-scale strike of coal miners took place in South Wales and the Government saw the absurdity of putting thousands of men in prison. The Labour Party and some union leaders accepted posts in the Government and this helped to raise the status of Labour and introduce changes in the industrial relations system. One of these changes was the Whitley system, which suggested that industrial councils could be formed in a number of industries to encourage worker participation in industry. The militants among the workers were suspicious, many employers were cool, and most councils disappeared in the chill economic recession of the early 1920s. The Industrial Courts Act of 1919 set up a permanent tribunal which was to survive for fifty years and settled many disputes. The Court was voluntary and the great majority of the parties accepted its decisions.

The industrial strike after the First World War brought a number of diagnoses from the employers. Looking at the period from the vantage point of the 1970s, we find the complaints familiar ones: 'frequent strikes or lockouts, restriction of output, wages per unit of value produced forced up to uneconomic heights, inflation of currency' and other related themes (D. A. Bremner *The Pathology of Industrial Unrest*, Engineers Association, London 1920). Mr Wedgwood Benn would be pleased to see an employer anticipating his 1972 strictures on the Press, as Mr Bremner writes 'sensational and grossly partisan journalism is a curse at the present time'. He ends by appealing for 'a general industrial armistice, whereby conditions would be stabilised for at least twelve months... which alone can save this country from economic disaster'.

The 'industrial armistice' did not materialise, but the strike rate fell after the failure of the miners and railwaymen to pursue joint strike tactics along with the Transport Workers, the so-called Triple Alliance. The falling strike rate was, however, due as much to the weak state of the economy as to the apparent decline in militancy. One explanation suggested by some is that the Labour Party polled well in the 1922 General Election and caused numbers of shop stewards and union officials to think more of changing society through the ballot box. Their hopes were rewarded in 1924, when a minority Labour government took office for a few months.

The General Strike of 1926

Industrial trouble flared again with the miners. The Conservative Government gave a subsidy to the mines in 1925 to avert a large scale strike. When the subsidy, which maintained wages, was withdrawn in April 1926, it precipitated the General Strike of May 1926, when the General Council of the TUC supported the striking miners. One and a half million men joined the million miners and industry was severely disrupted for several days, especially in transport, railways, docks, steel and power stations, the basic and important industries. The TUC tried to negotiate with the Government before the strike began and, at the Special Conference of the TUC from 29 April to 1 May, a resolution was moved by J. H. Thomas, MP supporting the efforts of 'the General Council to secure an honourable settlement of the differences in the coal mining industry'. Adjournments took place during the Conference so that the negotiating committee could confer with the Prime Minister, Mr Baldwin. They were faced with a refusal to move on miners' wages, and by Government arrangements for the organisation for maintenance of supplies (OMS). Ernest Bevin (Transport Workers), said that the unions on strike would arrange volunteer services to distribute essential food stuffs. He added 'We are not declaring war on the people. War has been declared by the Government, pushed on by sordid capitalism'. The miners had placed their case in the hands of the General Council, subject to consultation, and the Council wrote to the Prime Minister at the end of the Conference to say that the Government should negotiate with them. Two days later, on 3 May, the Government reply was that union instructions had gone out to start the strike on 4 May, and that 'overt acts had already taken place, including gross interference with the freedom of the Press. Such action involves a challenge to the constitutional rights and freedom of the nation'. The Press action was the refusal of the printers of the *Daily Mail* to print a leading article hostile to the strike. The strike began and the Government strategy was to present this sympathetic action (on behalf of the miners) as a challenge to law, order and the Constitution. After nine days the strike, which had widespread effects, was called off. The General Council stated that they had made some progress in negotiations but were hampered by the miners' slogan 'Not a minute on the day, not a penny off the pay'. The General Council's report on the strike, on which there were a number of recriminatory speeches, was passed by a majority of 3 to 1.

The aftermath

The General Strike was widely seen as a national challenge to the Government by organised labour, and represented a watershed in the history of the unions. The comparative failure of the strike led to a rise in discriminating action by employers ('victimisation') and a fall in union membership. This was reinforced by Parliamentary legislation to change the law on trade disputes in the following year.

The debate in Parliament focused on the nature of the General Strike. In May 1926, Sir John Simon argued

> A strike, properly understood, is perfectly lawful. The right to strike is the right of workmen in combination, by pre-arrangement, to give due notice to their employers to terminate their engagements, and to withhold their labour when these notices have expired (House of Commons, 6 May 1926).

He prefaced this by saying 'this so-called general strike is not a strike at all', on the grounds that it was 'an offence against the State and not a trade dispute in the sense of the Statute of 1906'. This view was reinforced by the judgement of Mr Justice Astbury in the High Court (Chancery) on 11 May in a dispute relating to the Sailors' and Firemen's Union.

> The so-called general strike... is illegal and contrary to law. ... No trade dispute has been alleged or shown to exist except in the miners' case, and no trade dispute can or does exist between the Trade Union Congress on the one hand and the Government and the nation on the other.

The 1927 Act had the intention of making a general strike illegal. A strike had to be confined to the industry in which the workers were engaged, and not for the purpose of bringing pressure on the Government. This seemed to rule out widespread sympathetic strikes, where one group of workers came out in support of another, and political strikes. Restrictions were put on Civil Service unions and Civil Servants. The result of this was to make it more difficult to predict how the law would view particular strikes, especially as the definition of 'intimidation' in picketing was widened

> ... to an extent which it is impossible to define, as it now includes causing in the mind of a person any apprehension of injury to him or his family in respect of his business, occupation, employment or source of income (W. H. Thompson in G. D. H. Cole *British Trade Unionism Today*, Methuen, London 1939, p. 125).

The combination of economic depression, falling union membership, the failure of militant unionism, and possibly the advent of the Labour Government in 1929–31, all combined to make the trade unions more conciliatory in their dealings with employers. This attitude was reinforced by the monetary crisis of 1931, the collapse of the minority Labour Government, the formation of a National (mainly Conservative) Government with a massive majority, and an unemployment level of some 3 million unemployed (about 20 per cent of the labour force) in early 1933. The strike rate fell dramatically after 1927 and during the 1930s strikes were small and usually unofficial. Union membership started to recover along with trade in the late 1930s and the newer industries, including cars, began to develop stronger unions.

In 1940, soon after the war had broken out, the Conditions of Employment and National Arbitration Order (Order 1305) was passed, making strikes and lockouts illegal unless attempts to settle the dispute had been made by arbitration or negotiation. Although there were a number of unofficial strikes, chiefly in mining, the low strike rate continued in wartime, as in peacetime. Strikers could be imprisoned, but this threat was put in cold storage after the famous and unsuccessful attempt to imprison and fine the leaders of the Kent miners in 1941. Order 1305 continued until 1951, when it was withdrawn, significantly after the failure of the Crown to prosecute unofficial strike leaders. The wartime Order 1305 had survived for six peacetime years, in spite of its restrictions on strikes, as it gave the unions a lever with which to force employers to the National Arbitration Tribunal. Another important reason was the landslide Labour victory of 1945, with Ernest Bevin as Foreign Secretary, that led to the repeal in 1946 of the 1927 Trade Disputes Act. In spite of Conservative promises in the late 1940s that they would, if returned to power, restore the 1927 Act, they did not sponsor major trade union legislation until 1970. The number of working days lost through disputes between 1946–57 was around 2½ million yearly. This compared well with the 1930s.

The post-war situation

The traditional system of collective bargaining, where employers and unions agreed nationally on wages and conditions, moved into a different social and economic framework. The massive unemployment of the 1919–39 period, which averaged some 14 per cent, virtually disappeared after 1945. While much of this was due to pent-up consumer demand, it was assisted by the work and writings of Lord Keynes, and made more widely known by Beveridge in his *Full Employment in a Free Society* (1944). Both political parties made public declarations of their belief in government counter-cyclical measures to maintain employment. While the Labour movement placed more faith in the ability of a Labour government to manage full employment and economic justice, the Conservatives continued on a prosperous course. While unemployment had disappeared as the major social scourge, it was now replaced by inflation. This made both the Labour and

Conservative governments more anxious to exercise a third party interest in the size and effect of wage bargaining.

Some economists argued that the new combination of full employment and free collective bargaining made stable prices impossible, and inflation would continue unless there was 'wage restraint' by the unions. The economic crisis of 1947, and the balance of payments difficulties, led the Labour Government to persuade the TUC to use its influence to moderate wage claims in 1948. The 'moderation' would apply to profits, prices and wages, so that all sections of the community would be affected. The policy continued throughout 1949 with considerable success, then disintegrated the following year because of the devaluation of the pound and the Korean War. Both these events led to strong 'cost-push' inflationary pressures which sent up prices in 1950 and 1951. The Conservative Chancellors in the 1950s were not successful in reaching agreement on wage restraint, and confined themselves to moral exhortations about 'moderation'. These appeals had little effect, as there was a shortage of labour and unions found it easy to settle with employers. At the same time, it would have been difficult for the moderate union leaders of the 1940s and 1950s, Arthur Deakin, Tom Williamson and William Lawther of the Transport Workers, General and Municipal Workers, and Mineworkers, to have advised wage restraint to their members. There were groups of militants at national and local level who could quickly channel resentment on particular issues. Some of these groups were Communists, whose influence was strong in the docks, electricity supply and engineering, in spite of the measures taken by some unions (for example, the Transport Workers) to debar them from holding union office. This was done by the democratic decision of delegates. In another case, a court case in which Byrne and Chapple of the ETU took legal proceedings against their union leadership, fraudulent electoral practices in the union were alleged. Mr Justice Winn ruled that the Communist leaders of the union 'conspired together to prevent by fraudulent and unlawful devices the election of the plaintiff Byrne in place of the defendant Haxell as General Secretary of the defendant's union' (ruling quoted in H. Pelling, op. cit., p. 252).

Numerous articles were written and radio and television commented on the influence of the Communists in fomenting industrial strife. This publicity, combined with the Hungarian rising of 1956, made the Communist cause unpopular in the middle and late 1950s. Yet industrial strife worsened after 1955 (see Table 1), showing that shop stewards of differing political and religious views would lead strikes if they felt deeply about the issue.

Although the strike figures in days lost were slightly higher in the 1950s than in the 1940s, there appeared to be a yearly figure of around 3 million in the early fifties and sixties which represented the real level. The greater mili-

TABLE 1
Strike figures for the 1950's

	No. of Stoppages	Working days lost through stoppages
1951	1,719	1,694,000
1952	1,714	1,792,000
1953	1,746	2,184,000
1954	1,989	2,457,000
1955	2,419	3,781,000
1956	2,648	2,083,000
1957	2,859	8,412,000
1958	2,629	3,462,000
1959	2,093	5,270,000
1960	2,849	3,024,000

tancy in 1957 accounted for the highest yearly figure of days lost through strikes since 1926, showing that one lengthy strike with thousands of workers taking part pushes up the figures dramatically.

Nevertheless, the relatively low number of days lost showed either (a) that the unions were less militant, or (b) that the employers conceded most of their wage demands and, in an inflationary situation, passed on the rise in prices to the consumer, who in turn asked for higher wages. Some economists argued that the inflation was primarily due to excess supply of money by the Government, plus excessive public expenditures, and that inflation was primarily 'demand-pull' with workers chasing higher prices by asking for higher wages.

The changing pattern of strikes

Although the 'days lost' figure was low, the number of stoppages increased greatly, showing the shift in power from the national union to the local shop steward. By the middle and late 1960s, nearly 95 per cent of all disputes were unofficial, as shop stewards found that a short strike was an effective way of resolving a dispute with an employer. The number of strikes by itself does not show the inflationary pressure, as many employers settled quickly to avoid the threat of a strike. This increase in unofficial strikes took place from the mid 1950s at a time when other trade competitors (such as Sweden and

Germany) suffered less lost time through strikes. A high number of strikes had reasons other than wages as their stated cause; dismissals, redundancies, manning, restrictive practices, discipline – all these areas of trouble show the period of transition through which some areas of industry were passing. Although employment was high, there was structural unemployment in the older basic industries of mining, shipbuilding, textiles and railways.

Old skills became obsolescent, in spite of the unions' insistence on craft training, and machines replaced jobs previously done by hand. These trends made the unions resistant to change in industry, although there were Government re-training schemes. Miners went on strike, not to close mines, but to keep them open against Coal Board efforts to close uneconomic ones. The dockers, after years of guerilla fighting against containerisation, finally erupted in a national strike, caused partly by the Industrial Relations Act of 1971.

It is ironic to consider, in the middle of the great debate about the role of law and industrial relations, that by 1950 the British public was deeply concerned, according to newspapers and opinion pollsters, about strikes, and this at a time when the days lost through strikes were one seventh or one eight of the total in 1972. In 1959, a Gallup Poll 'reported that, in twenty-two years of polling, criticism of the unions among the rest of the public had never been higher' (*Trade Unions in a Changing Society*', PEP, London 1963, p. 207). This public criticism was partly due to inconvenience or discomfort suffered through strikes, particularly bus, rail and dock strikes, which are widely publicised and reported almost daily. Newspapers, radio and television see industrial relations only when there is disruption; good industrial relations is not news. Another factor was the changing status of the industrial worker, who now had a wage comparable to, and sometimes better than, the white collar employee. The traditional middle class, and aspiring middle class, saw their salary differentials being eroded. As one young teacher said, 'lorry drivers earn more than I do'. The white collar, lower middle class employee was often on a salary that was slow to adjust to price and wage changes, for which inflation the unions were held by many to be primarily responsible. Mass education completed the erosion of the white collar differential, as the larger numbers of potential clerical and administrative workers reduced their comparative earnings against those of the manual worker who was in a stronger bargaining position.

While Mr Macmillan and the Conservatives won the 1959 General Election on the slogan 'You never had it so good', many citizens continued to feel aggrieved with trade union strikers, even with the relatively modest strike figures of the early 1960s. The public, or newspapers claiming to speak for the public, drew attention to a range of other worker or union activities, such as the 'go-slow', 'work-to-rule', overtime ban, 'withdrawal of co-operation' and other methods aimed at making a factory uneconomic or a public service unuseable. The 'wildcat' strike began to be headlined in the newspapers, so that any unofficial stoppage, or over 90 per cent of all disputes, were reported as 'another wildcat'. The word found its way into descriptions of the Contracts of Employment Bill in December 1962. One reporter hailed this as 'Wildcat strikes take a slap' and wrote, after describing the mutual obligations of contract, that

> any worker with two years service who goes on strike will break his continuous employment and he forfeits his statutory rights if he goes on strike without giving 14 days notice of it.
>
> With this proposal adding a new penalty to those who take part in lightning strikes – both official and unofficial – Mr Hare has satisfied the demands of a group of Tory M.P.'s. (*Daily Express*, 13 December 1962).

We see here the beginnings of government action to stop unofficial strikes, as this experienced labour correspondent, Trevor Evans, considered this Bill as 'probably the most serious effort yet to stifle lightning strikes'. The Conservatives in the 1950s had pinned their hopes on a free economy and free collective bargaining, defined as the absence of government control, but this foundered on the periodic financial crisis, such as the aftermath of Suez. In this situation the engineering employers had intended to resist the wage claim of their unions, but they failed to get the Government backing which they had expected. The Government conciliated and compromised (see H. A. Clegg and R. Adams *The Employers' Challenge*, Blackwell, Oxford 1957). Curiously enough, in view of the continued criticism of bad industrial relations by the Conservative Opposition in Parliament in the 1964–70 period, and of many of their back-benchers over the post-war period, the Conservatives did not set up a Royal Commission to report on industrial relations when they were in power from 1951 to 1964. Mr Wilson points out that 'Mr Heath, as Minister of Labour, had in 1960 specifically rejected a back-bench proposal for an inquiry' (H. Wilson *The Labour Government 1964–70*, Weidenfeld, London 1971, p. 538).

Government concern over unofficial strikes was linked to an attempt, the first since the Labour Government wage policy of 1948, to set a norm or 'guiding light' of $2\frac{1}{2}$ per cent on pay and salary increases in the public sector. It was hoped that this would set a Spartan example to employers in the private sector of industry but, as was to happen again and again in the next ten years, the policy of 'sitting hard' on the public employees did not work. Private sector wages and salaries rose well above the 'guiding light', while nurses, teachers and others demonstrated in the streets at what they thought to be unfair treatment. Like an Edwardian novelette, 'The Light that Failed', the economy revived, and the public sector began to regain its relative wage position.

The Government showed its conversion from its basic free enterprise stance by setting up the National Economic Development Commission (Neddy), to plan for economic growth in the manner of some successful West European examples; in the field of wages and salaries, the National Incomes Commission (NIC) was set up. The TUC agreed to serve on Neddy, as they approved of attempts to stimulate economic growth, but they refused to sit on NIC, claiming that its aim was to curb pay increases; as George Woodcock put it, it was 'setting a lad to do a man's job'. Nonetheless, Neddy and NIC represented an important change in attitude for Conservatives and they provided the embryo framework for the more detailed and comprehensive wages, prices and productivity plans of the 1964 Labour Government.

The incomes policy of the Labour Government did not work as smoothly or successfully as they had hoped in the pre-election years of 1962–63. The unions had accepted the policy with some reluctance, as it brought a third party interest into the confrontation between employers and unions. There was also the traditional union suspicion that an incomes policy was a wage restraint policy. These doubts reverberated through the Conferences, and were finally resolved when the TUC accepted a resolution supporting 'the planned growth of incomes'. If the 1964 Labour Government had not faced an inflationary situation, a rapidly growing balance of payments deficit and an international 'run on the pound', then planned growth of incomes might have been possible. But the sterling crisis forced the Government to restrict credit, raise taxes and slow down economic growth. Real income rose relatively slowly as prices rose quickly and the incomes 'norm' of $3 - 3\frac{1}{2}$ per cent pressed heavily on union pay claims. Harold Wilson writes of the dilemma 'the underpaid railwaymen had a strong case' while as a Prime Minister he thought that 'to yield incontinently to strike threats would mean the end of any meaningful prices and incomes policy, with serious effects abroad' (Wilson, *op. cit.*, p. 199). The last thought was the decisive one, as it led to the March 1966 General Election. Mr Wilson saw himself as the final negotiator in the Government line on five occasions. Significantly, two of his interventions preceded General Elections, in February 1966 with the railwaymen, and in June 1970 with the newspaper strike. The third important intervention was the Liverpool dock strike of October 1967, 'the damage from which aggravated the foreign exchange movements which forced devaluation' (Wilson, *op cit.*, p. 209).

The mind of Mr Wilson and his Cabinet became increasingly occupied with the question of the damaging strike. The seamen's strike in mid 1966 caused serious balance of payments difficulties as it lasted seven weeks. The

Government blamed strong Communist pressure within the Seamen's Union for the continuance and bitterness of the strike. Yet, even at this stage, the Labour Government did not intend to pass legislation to make it more difficult for unions to strike, or in discourage unofficial strikers. The problem was tackled by announcing a six months 'standstill' on incomes and prices, to be followed by six months of severe restraint. The standstill was breached by ASSET (Association of Supervisory Staffs, Executives and Technicians) who backed one of their members against Thorn Electrical Industries for breach of promise to pay a wage increase.

The main loopholes in the pay 'standstill' were plugged, and there were no important court cases. By mid 1967, Mr. Lee, Chancellor of the Duchy of Lancaster, was saying that there had been widespread voluntary acceptance of the 'freeze' and that this proved that 'the tough prices and incomes policy was reasonable and fair.' There had been only 14 minor cases of the use of compulsory powers, affecting only 36,000 workers in a working population of some 23 million. (See *The Guardian*, 31 July 1967).

2 Proposals for Changes in Trade Union Law

Predictably, the very high strike figures of 8 million working days lost in 1957, along with the London bus strike of 1958, brought a demand for changes in the law relating to trade unions. The Inns of Court Conservative and Unionist Society produced a book entitled *A Giant's Strength* to outline their proposals for reform. They argued that a tribunal should look into restrictive practices, for example practices which employ more men and waste more time than are necessary for the task in hand, and that it should be a punishable offence to carry on a restrictive practice which has been declared contrary to the public interest by a tribunal. Little seems to have come of this suggestion as the 1971 Act did not advocate this.

The proposals also dealt with the question of 'unfair' expulsion from union membership. In some trades, occupations or industries loss of union membership means loss of job. The case of Bonsor *v.* Musicians Union, where Bonsor's expulsion meant he could not work in the musical world, is an example of this.

The 'cooling-off' period made its appearance in the suggestions. Strikes should only be started fourteen days after a tribunal has outlined the facts to the public. The USA and Canada are cited as examples of countries where the 'cooling-off' device is used. It is argued that this would do much to prevent the lightning or unofficial strike over demarcation; victimisation or redundancy would be hindered or prevented.

Registration for unions is proposed, with the lifting of immunity for actions in tort for those unions who refuse to register. This would lay them open to action by employers or others for breach of contract. Finally, the powers of the TUC should be strengthened.

The Conservative proposals for reform were developed further in April 1968, and appeared some months before the publication of the Donovan Report as *Fair Deal at Work*. The Conservative approach to modern industrial relations argued that collective bargaining should be responsible, and agreements should be kept. From this beginning would flow industrial peace and greater efficiency.

The cornerstone of their reforms was to be an Industrial Relations Act, embracing present trade union law and bringing in desirable new features. Much of this seems to have been borrowed from existing US legislation. There was to be a Registrar of Trade Unions and Employers Associations, with compulsory registration to ensure that union rules were acceptable and fair to members. This would have the effect of making unions corporate bodies, which would then exist in law and be liable for torts 'except in the circumstances of a lawful trade dispute'. It follows that a lawful strike would be capable of definition, and certain kinds of strikes, such as inter-union or sympathetic ones, would become illegal. The concept of the 'national emergency strike', borrowed from US legislation, also appears. Strikes that would damage the national economy would be referred to a Board of Inquiry and then to the Industrial Court. This reference could be made without the agreement of the parties, and an injunction could be made with a view to preventing strikes or industrial action.

The case is made that some industrial trouble springs from insecurity and workers should have more security of employment. This had been foreshadowed by the Contracts of Employment Act 1964, and the Redundancy Payments Act 1965. Protection would be given to the individual worker against expulsion from his union, subject to scrutiny of the rules. Expelled members should usually have the chance to continue in the same employment, unless their expulsion was for non-payment of union dues.

An Industrial Court, with High Court status, would be created. This would be the court where applications for injunctions would be heard and issued, as well as the applications in the case of national emergency disputes.

The differences between the suggestions made in *Fair Deal at Work* and the Donovan Report differ on a number of points. As we shall see, *Fair Deal* proposes that trade unions accept responsibility for the actions of their members, and is more confident that a legal framework for industrial relations will lead to more stable relations and industrial peace. We can now contrast this with the views of the Donovan Report.

The Donovan Report

The Donovan Commission focused its attention on strikes as a major sign of disruption in industrial relations, above all the high percentage of unofficial strikes (95 per cent of all strikes) which took place. Critics of the British system of 'voluntarism' argued that legal restrictions on strike activity seemed to have some success in other countries. Germany and Sweden were mentioned amongst the countries with low strike figures and a framework of labour law, while among the countries with an Anglo-Saxon system of law, the United States and Australia both had restrictions on strikes, although their strike figures were comparatively high.

The Commission further defined the unofficial strike: 'our problem is the short spontaneous outburst' lasting 'an average of $2\frac{1}{2}$ days'. The existing law allowed the employer to take such strikers to court. This was seldom done; apart from the costs and publicity involved, the case would be heard after the dispute had been ended or settled, and the resulting bad feeling might affect the work situation.

One suggestion considered was the 'peace' clause in a collective bargaining contract. Both parties to the contract should agree not to strike or lock out during the term of the contract. The 'peace' clause would include the promise not to use other sanctions against the other party. There would be no disputes halting production, which would be of benefit to employers in highly capitalised or mass production industries. This is in line with US practice, where the contract is for one or two years, and unions undertake to settle disputes by arbitration as a last resort. The problem for Britain is the question of the enforceability of such clauses.

As the Commission states, 'in this country collective agreements are not legally binding contracts', though there is no legal reason why employers and workers could not sign such contracts. They do not sign them because they have a preference for collective bargaining as a process rather than a contract. Another difficulty is identifying which group on the employee side is the 'party' to the contract, as this could be the national union officials, the district officials, or the shop stewards. This fragmentation of responsibility makes legal enforcement through court action uncertain in its effect. This was clearly shown in the Ford case of early 1969, when the Ford Co. took the T and GWU to the High Court for breach of a collective bargaining contract, only to discover that a contract was only legally enforceable when it was drawn up and signed by the parties with possible legal enforceability in mind. Contracts would also have to be drafted with more legal precision, a job for lawyers rather than negotiators. The heart of the problem of unofficial and unconstitutional strikes is summed up in the words 'those who would be bound by the agreements do not break them in any court, and those who are in the habit of breaking them would not be bound' (Donovan Report, p. 129). The first part of the quotation relates to the union, which rarely takes unconstitutional action; the second part to the members, who do.

This brings us to the problem of the enforceability of law in industrial relations. The Commission points out that agreements signed by unions may be voted down by members, and that new members entering the firm or industry are not necessarily bound by the agreements. (To a non-lawyer the second argument seems strange; a new entrant knows that the agreement exists, and accepts this as part of his conditions of work or service. The first argument has practical as well as legal substance.)

If sanctions are not to be directed against unions acting as agents for their members, the alternative step is to make the individual worker responsible for breach of contract. The Report argues that this was unworkable even in wartime (i.e. 1940–45), when strikes were virtually forbidden under Order 1305. This was breached by the Kent miners and the leaders had to be released from prison, while those who were fined did not pay. Unofficial strikes were more frequent in wartime than in the 1930s. Both Conservative and Labour parties in the wartime Coalition Government agreed that jail and imprisonment was ineffective if large numbers defied the order not to strike.

The Commission was not 'in principle opposed to the use of legal sanctions for the enforcement of agreed procedures' but 'sanctions will remain unworkable until a fundamental change in our system of industrial relations has led to a situation in which employers may be able and willing to use such rights as the law gives them'. There follows the prophetic statement, which summed up the dilemma in which the Conservative Government found itself in 1972, 'at the present time legislation making procedure agreements legally enforceable would not in fact be enforced, and like all legislation that is not enforced would bring the law into disrepute' (Donovan Report, p. 136). The way out of the legal dilemma is through the reform of collective bargaining. 'Britain has two systems of collective bargaining. The one is the formal system embodied in the official institutions. The other is the informal system created by the actual behaviour of trade unions and employers' associations, of managers, shop stewards and workers'. (Donovan Report, p.12). The two systems create instability, profit from inflation and labour shortage, and through 'wage drift' cause earnings to rise more quickly than wage rates and far more quickly than productivity. The loose, informal arrangements at factory level make for conflict. New and comprehensive collective bargaining arrangements would be needed at factory level to deal with terms and situations which arise and must be settled there.

It was suggested that boards of companies should review and revise their industrial relations with regard to six objectives: to reform collective bargaining machinery so that it becomes more 'comprehensive and authoritative'; develop machinery for settling grievances quickly and fairly; regularise the position of shop stewards; make agreements about redundancy; develop rules and procedures on discipline at work; plan regular joint discussion on safety matters. For their part, employers should welcome the right of employees to join unions, and should also collect statistics and other information which may, if necessary, be offered to workers' representatives.

The Commission recommends that an Industrial Relations Act should be passed. When the collective bargaining agreements have been improved, as suggested above, they should be registered with the Department of Employment and Productivity (DEP). This will establish the responsibility of the board of directors for industrial relations, and also make possible an official overview of such agreements to see whether they are 'clear and firm'. Sanctions are favoured, 'a monetary penalty' if companies (initially over 5,000 employees) either do not register agreements or report no agreements.

A statutory body should also to be set up, an Industrial Relations Commission (IRC) 'to investigate and report upon cases and problems arising out of the registration of agreements' and other matters in industrial relations. The DEP should continue to deal with problems until such time as they needed to be passed on to the IRC.

The proposal for a public body to 'hear recognition disputes and make recommendations for their settlement' is found in the evidence of Allan Flanders to the Donovan Commission. This permanent body would have its own staff who could carry out inquiries and conduct secret ballots (to some extent the proposal resembles the NLRB, US National Labour Relations Board). It could deal with jurisdictional disputes where rival unions claim representation over the same group of workers. Procedural disputes over 'closed shop', unfair practices or facilities and security for representatives could be best handled by this tribunal, which would give reasons for decisions made and build up a body of principles or case law. Flanders suggests that when a dispute is referred to this tribunal an embargo, backed by financial penalties, should be imposed on strikes or lockouts by the parties to the dispute. However, voluntary acceptance of the tribunal's findings would be preferable to monetary sanctions.

The Donovan Commission accepted the idea of a permanent body, which would be guided by the principle that collective bargaining is the bedrock of industrial relations, that this depends on strong trade unions, and that there should be clear and precise written agreements, with a pay structure to match.

Other proposals of the Commission included the gradual replacement of wages councils by collective bargaining, and making contracts saying that employees should not belong to an illegal trade union. This was another example of 'borrowing' from US legislation, as the Wagner Act of 1933 forbade the 'yellow dog' contract by which an employee stated that he was not a trade unionist. Protection against unfair dismissal, unless for good cause, was to be ensured by legislation and heard by the present industrial tribunals. Finally, the individal union member was to be protected against unfair expulsion from his union, or against unfair exclusion. Union rules would have to meet certain standards as a condition of registration law.

TUC evidence to the Donovan Commission

The reaction of the TUC to the Donovan Report should be seen against the proposals which it placed before the Commission. TUC evidence in relation to industrial conflict stated that an absence of strikes or disputes was not necessarily good industrial relations, and that days lost through strikes in

Britain 'is consistently much lower than in most other industrial economies'. The evidence was true in 1966, when presented, but was far from being true in 1972, when the days lost had risen seven or eightfold. An examination of the causes of strikes in 1960 showed that 32 per cent of strikes were over money, 21 per cent over dismissals, and 6 per cent over 'recognition, non-unionism, breaking agreements' and so on (TUC *Evidence*, 2nd edn, January 1967). The unions pointed out that much of the responsibility for strikes was the employers', although the workers were usually blamed, and the press publicised the unions as the villains. A more welcoming attitude to unions was needed and procedure agreements should be widened in scope. Unofficial strikes were said to be greatly exaggerated, as half those reported ended by being made official. Inconsistencies in the public demand for strikers to be disciplined were seen, as the public dislikes seeing non-strikers or rule breakers disciplined by the union. The TUC stressed that industrial relations in Britain had been built up by the unions, and state interference had been left to a minimum, with some success.

The TUC were cool on the issue of Labour Courts, which related to a different system of industrial relations from the voluntaristic system in Britain. It attached more importance to legislation preventing unfair dismissal, which it claimed led to 230 stoppages of work in 1965. It suggested an extension of the clear and written procedures in the public sector to the private sector. The unions objected to the legal enforcement of collective agreements. Instead of Britain's needing to borrow legal provisions from other systems, it was the other countries that envied our 'generally enlightened approach to industrial relations' and our absence of legal coercion. Following this line, the TUC wanted the 1906 Act (breached by Rookes *v.* Barnard, making breach of contract actionable through 'the re-discovery of the tort of civil intimidation') rewritten to read: 'An act done in pursuance of an agreement or combination by two or more persons shall, if done in contemplation of furtherance of a trade dispute, not be actionable unless the act, if done without any such agreement or combination, would be actionable. *In a trade dispute, breach of contract cannot give rise to the tort of conspiracy*' (*op. cit.* p. 183). The law of peaceful picketing should be extended to include vehicles, and the definition of an 'industrial dispute' should be amended under a wider meaning embracing disputes between employers and workmen, or between workmen and workmen.

TUC Reaction to Donovan*

The first criticism was one made by others; that the 'two systems of industrial

* TUC *Action on Donovan*, Interim Statement, November 1968.

28

relations' oversimplified the complex structure of collective bargaining in British industry, and generalised from the experience of two industries, engineering and building. There was a guarded welcome for the Commission on Industrial Relations (CIR), provided that there were an exchange of information between Joint Industrial Councils (JICs) and the CIR. Judgements of the CIR should not be binding or collective bargaining would wither under the threat of sanctions. The CIR should deal with procedural agreements, on the making and definition of contracts, rather than substantive agreements, which deal with the issues of negotiation and need 'continuous handling'. The TUC agreed that the CIR could investigate trade union recognition.

The TUC shared the Donovan views on freedom of association, and the non-enforceability of collective agreements, which 'would be both undesirable and impracticable'. The unions said that changing technology, for instance in the car industry, needed continuous negotiation and not legal enforceability. Procedures should be improved and good procedures should be followed conscientiously. The TUC was satisfied with the Donovan position on strikes and the law on trade disputes, and agreed that 'cooling off' periods and compulsory strike ballots were not useful. It felt that the Commission should have recommended greater protection 'in relation to disputes about trade union recognition' where doubts may exist. Agreement was expressed with Donovan on picketing and conspiracy, but disagreement about the need for unions to register compulsorily. It welcomed the Commission's refusal to prohibit the 'closed shop', and agreed with the need to have greater protection against unfair dismissal. Caution was felt about the proposal for Labour Tribunals, although the existing Industrial Tribunals could have their jurisdiction extended. There was, it was said, no need for appeals to the High Court, provided that the Tribunals were 'informal' and 'conciliatory'. Significantly, the TUC held to its general view that there was no need 'for all chairmen to be legally qualified'. This was contrary to the Donovan view, which would have legal chairmen ruling on points of law.

The TUC reaction was a comparatively sober one, given the view of the union militants, (close to that of the Communist Party pamphlet *Donovan Exposed* which said 'this is a most dangerous report, basically acceding to reactionary demands'). The Report, the Communists said, was designed as an attack on earnings, as it spoke approvingly of an incomes policy, and wanted to end the fragmentation of collective bargaining which leads to 'leap-frogging' of wage claims and 'wage drift' of earnings upwards. The Donovan statement that 95 per cent of all strikes were unofficial was stood neatly on its head by the Communist statement; 'the Commission advocates, for the first time in over half a century, that 95 percent of all strikes taking place in this country should be made illegal'. The pamphlet ends with the call for the working class movement to 'resist this onslaught'.

Press comment on Donovan

The reception by the Press of the Donovan Report varied across the political spectrum. The militant left were critical, although Mr Frank Cousins gave a 'guarded welcome', and the right wing newspapers were disappointed that a firm legal approach was missing. The centre left and centre right gave the Report a cordial welcome. *The Times* talked of the clear and authoritative diagnosis, and of the middle ground chosen between the 'legalist' and 'traditional' schools of industrial relations. The IRC was said to be 'a somewhat fuzzy body' with a 'lack of teeth', but the Donovan proposals were on the right lines. *The Observer* comment was on much the same lines, but it took the opportunity of the railway dispute in summer 1968, and the railmen's go-slow to point out that the good intentions of Donovan were often only 'hopeful noises', and did little to solve inter-union disputes.

The academic view was put by one of the leading men in the field of industrial relations, Mr Allen Flanders, though he and his colleagues at Oxford and Warwick are sometimes accused of over-influencing the Commission to the Oxford School viewpoint. He welcomed the Report's proposals to 'make the future of collective bargaining its foremost concern', and the reform of collective bargaining the first priority. He said that the employers had chosen to deal with the powerful work groups led by shop stewards rather than the trade union officials. This was the reality of shop floor power, but it fragmented the collective bargaining system to the point of anarchy, as the Report put it. Unofficial strikes were the symptom of this disorder, and the way to improvement lay in the reform of bargaining machinery and procedures. He agreed with the emphasis on voluntary reform, though he supported the Commission's proposals for statutory legal safeguards against unfair dismissal, and a review body 'with legal powers' to handle complaints of members against unions. Flanders agreed with the Commission's stand against the legal enforcement of collective contracts; 'to enforce present procedural agreements when they are neither clear nor effective would not only be unreasonable, in most cases it would be impossible' (*The Times* 14 June 1968). This last statement is the classic position of those who support the voluntaristic system: improve bargaining procedures, re-draft the scope of the agreement, then it might be possible to move forward to bilateral agreement on legal enforcement.

A more critical view of Donovan came from the industrialists and managers. Mr Dewdney, a managing director and one time deputy chairman of the Prices and Incomes Board, wrote that 'unofficial strikes arise from the imbalance of power, and are inflated, not created, by the lack of negotiating machinery' (*The Times*, 8 August 1968). From this followed a plea for more competition and cost-consciousness in industry, which would compel management to negotiate keenly with unions, and an implicit call for a legal framework for the collective contract. Another managing director, from the car industry, said that Donovan did not take things much further forward and called for 'discouragement of unofficial stoppages, keeping wage increases in line with productivity, ensuring that agreements are honoured'. This is more a statement of objectives than a programme for action. We are not told what 'discouraged' means, or how one 'ensures' that agreements are kept; presumably by law, and it was to fill this power vacuum that the Conservative Party advocated their code of industrial relations.

Mr Robert Carr accused the Donovan Report of inconsistency. He said everyone agreed that our system of industrial relations needed change but 'the chief argument concerns the role of law' and the British system needs to be brought into line with other large industrial nations who have 'a comprehensive framework of legislation'. Throughout his article (*The Times* 31 July 1968) Mr Carr argues for legislation instead of voluntarism. and he quotes the US and Canada as examples of legislation in a democracy. He wants to 'put the concept of the binding agreement right in the centre of the bargaining table'. Obedience to the law is an attitude of mind and not the threat of legal sanctions, or 'preventive medicine' as Mr. Carr terms it.

The discussion which followed the publication of the Donovan Report showed clearly, even in 1968, how the battle lines of the 1970s were to be drawn; the unions wanting as little law as possible, and freely negotiated agreements; the industrialists asking for agreements to be honoured, and pointing to the damage caused by the growing number of unofficial strikes; the Conservatives, then in Opposition, arguing that a legal framework for industrial relations would make a powerful contribution to industrial stability, and force unions to think responsibly about binding contracts.

3 The Labour Government and Industrial Relations Reform

The need for legislation arising from the Donovan Report had to be faced by the Labour Government by early 1969. There were two main reasons for this: the number of unofficial strikes was increasing year by year and getting a great deal of publicity in the Press; prices were rising rapidly along with wages and the resultant inflation put pressure on the Government to take action. The Government were sensitive to such criticism as they had been forced to devalue the pound in late 1967. Some of the strikes in the head lines were of the kind which made the Press and the public demand that 'something should be done'. They were of the infamous 'who does what' variety, linked in the public mind with disputes over who bores the holes or puts in the screws. The Girling brake dispute, which cost the car industry millions of pounds, lasted four weeks in late 1968. It was an example of a strike by a handful of men which puts thousands out of work. A member of one union turned off an oil valve said to be the 'job property' of another union. This became an inter-union dispute and the disputed machinery was declared 'black'. Suspension of workers led to the strike. This dispute under-lined the weakness of the voluntary system when faced by a stubborn refusal to agree to follow negotiating procedures. Other disputes followed, trivial in their issues, but laying off hundreds of workers over car parking disputes or office cleaners.

There were also threats of strike action in the steel industry as both the Steelworkers (I & STC) and the ASTMS claimed jurisdiction over white collar staff, with the latter union seeking to penetrate deeply into what had been the domain of the I & STC. The fear of having an important industry closed down at a time of financial crisis for the country led to a Commission of Inquiry under Lord Pearson. There were further disputes over the findings of the Inquiry. All these disputes in key industries, cars, steel and engineering, focused the government's mind on the problem of stability in industrial relations.

The appearance of Mrs Barbara Castle in mid 1968 as the Secretary of State for Employment and Productivity brought the need for change and the catalyst together. By January 1969 a White Paper, 'In Place of Strife', had been published, which set out the virtues and vices of the industrial relations system. It followed one of the Donovan themes: 'it [the system] has produced a growing number of lightning strikes and contributed little to increasing efficiency....Radical changes are needed... to meet the needs of a period of rapid technical and industrial change'. In discussing the role of the government in industrial relations, the paper said that 'the State has always been involved in the process of industrial relations. It has always had to provide a framework of law'. There had been two approaches by the State: the doctrine of 'collective *laisser-faire*' with the Government standing aloof from the conflict; the more modern view, that the Government 'should intervene... if it could be shown that certain important economic or social objectives were not sufficiently furthered or were frustrated by collective bargaining'. The examples chosen here were a restriction on strikes which hinder unduly essential services, life or property; the Contracts of Employment Act and Redundancy Payments Scheme.

The need for a positive approach being proven, what should be done? The paper followed the Donovan Report in suggesting the reform of collective bargaining to improve untidy or chaotic agreements which were 'too slow, too informal and too uncertain' to provide the basis for the orderly settlement of grievances. It recommended that a Commission on Industrial Relations (CIR) be established. This would be an independent body, which would examine trade union claims for recognition; help reform trade unions; assist companies and unions to negotiate suitable agreements in cases where failure has been reported. A wide variety of information about industrial relations would have to be collected. The DEP should keep a register of agreements, firstly on a voluntary, then on a statutory basis.

Thus far the White Paper followed the Donovan thesis closely, but it diverged on the role of law in collective agreements. Agreements could be made legally binding, if the parties desired this. Management would have to provide more information to assist in the development and extension of collective bargaining. The controversial differences appeared in the law relating to strikes and the national interest. Strikes in breach of national procedure were usually lightning strikes, so a 'conciliation pause' was recommended, during which a solution would be sought in twenty-eight days. During this period both sides should observe specified terms of employment (pp. 28–9 of the White Paper). Strike ballots were also suggested, implying that militant union leaders might be out of touch with shop floor opinion. There were to be safeguards against unfair dismissal with statutory backing. Complaints against unions or employers could be heard by an Industrial Board, which might decree a financial penalty, though there would be no imprisonment for default.

Mr George Woodcock, General Secretary of the TUC, was named chairman of the CIR in January, but the TUC attitude to the proposed reforms was hostile. The objections were mainly about the compulsory ballots, the 'conciliation pause' or 'cooling-off' period, and the threat of fines. Mr

Feather, then Assistant General Secretary of the TUC, said the proposals were unworkable, undesirable and unnecessary. With uncanny foresight he predicted 'if two or three thousand dockers in Liverpool or Hull or London struck and were fired... they would refuse to pay. An employer would be required then to deduct the fine from each docker's wages and a new strike would start' (*The Times*, 4 February 1969). Later events were to prove him right, with five dockers serving instead of three thousand.

Some commentators have argued that, if the Cabinet had met and agreed to pass an Act on the lines of the White Paper, the majority of Labour MPs would have supported it, and certainly the Conservatives would as well. Public opinion was shown by opinion pools to be strongly in favour of such a measure. In the event, the TUC objections led to growing back-bench Labour MP pressure on Cabinet and Parliament, in spite of the repeated statements by Mr Wilson and Mrs Castle that a new Act was needed. In March 1969, Mrs. Castle was moving the approval of the White Paper 'In Place of Strife' 'as a basis for legislation' and inviting 'Her Majesty's Government to continue consultation with a view to preparing legislation' (House of Commons debates. 3 March 1969). The main aim was to reform collective bargaining by improving procedures and agreements. Employers who refuse to negotiate, after the CIR has dealt with the complaint, can be taken to 'binding arbitration of the industrial court'. In some industries, she continued 'we are getting very near anarchy' and men 'down tools' too readily and strike. A conciliation pause was needed, as the dismissal of a few men could throw thousands out of work. She accused the Tories and some employers of insisting that all collective agreements be made legally enforceable, which would make matters worse, not better. The nub of the opposition to her proposals centred around 'the proposal for attachment of earnings' or the levying of fines, though this had been put forward to prevent workers being imprisoned in lieu of fines.

Mr Carr, for the Opposition, reiterated his theme that collective agreements, once made. should be honoured. He singled out the twin diseases of British industrial relations, lightning strikes and inflationary wage increases. He said wage agreements should be made freely and 'to attempt to control wages by law is futile... it undermines the authority of official union leadership and it stimulates militancy and causes injustice'. The immunity of trade unions under, or, as Mr Carr put it, 'above the law' was given them so that they could bargain equally with employers. 'It was not given to them ...in order to fight each other, to enforce a closed shop, to improve secondary boycotts on other people or to break agreements'. Much of Mr Carr's speech foreshadowed the changes which the Conservatives were to introduce over three years later, although his gift of prophecy failed him when he forecast that their 1970s' Industrial Relations Act would be as 'warmly welcomed as was the Act of the 1870s by the TUC of that day'. The Conservatives opposed the Labour Government's White Paper as it lacked 'a modern system of civil law'.

Labour members who opposed the White Paper dealt mainly with three issues, the compulsory strike ballot, the conciliation pause, and the attachment of earnings. The vote showed that the Conservatives had abstained, leaving 224 Labour MPs supporting the Government line and 63 MPs against, with some Labour abstentions. The dissentient Labour MPs were acting as the spokesmen for the trade union point of view.

A characteristic pamphlet opposing 'In Place of Strife' came from the Draughtsmen and Allied Technicians Association (DATA) which told its members that 'hard won rights were in danger'. The main force of its attack was on the impracticability of legally binding contracts, backed by fines for breach of contract, along with strike ballots and compulsory trade union registration.

The Ford case

Overshadowing the White Paper debate, although the matter was *subjudice*, was the silent major premise of the Ford dispute, where the matter at issue was the legal status of the collective bargaining agreement. There was a joint negotiating committee at Fords, with a representative from each of the fifteen unions. This committee had conducted joint negotiations for several years and in 1969 Ford negotiated a 'no-strike' clause as part of a new agreement. This was agreed by a small majority on the worker side of the committee. When the terms were made public (for instance, that strikes which ignored procedure could lead to a loss of 'lay off' pay and holiday bonus), the shop stewards and militant workers organised meetings and strikes. Ford applied for an injunction, and sued the union for breach of contract.

The case showed the difficulty of enforcing a collective bargaining contract at law. The Ford Co. did not sue the shop stewards or individual strikers (over 30,000) but the union itself. The question was, did the negotiating committee agreement bind the unions concerned? The loose negotiating procedures in British industry were shown clearly here: the joint committee concluded an agreement, but the dissentients, including the powerful Engineers and the Transport Workers, did not approve. More importantly, the shop stewards and a majority of the workers did not approve either, and had the power to call a strike. If the worker reaction had not taken place, the national unions would have ratified the agreement as a matter of form. In fact, the T & GWU voted originally to accept, then later opposed, the agreement. The AEF (Amalgamated Union of Engineering and Foundry Workers) declared the unofficial strike official and were followed a day later by the T & GWU.

The crux of the matter was that if the negotiating committee had sought the opinion of the shop stewards (the great majority of workers were AEF or T & WU) the 'no strike' clause would have been refused. The unofficial strike was the chief weapon of the shop stewards in levering up pay, and pay statistics showed their immense success with this tactic. This is why management wanted the 'no unconstitutional strike' clause. The injunction showed the ineffectiveness of the law against large numbers as the strikers defied the injunction and the strike continued. After two weeks the case Ford Motor Co. Ltd. *v.* Amalgamated Union of Engineering and Foundry Workers and Transport and General Workers Union, was heard.

The case centred around the argument 'when is an agreement an agreement?' and the answer appeared to be 'When it was intended to be by the signatories'. No such intention (in a legal sense) appeared in the Ford agreement signed by the committee (NJNC). This was a 'gentleman's agreement', said to be morally but not legally binding. If made by parties who are not 'gentlemen' then it can be broken if it is to the advantage of one party. This happened in the Ford case. A layman looking at the agreement would have said that it looked straightforward: the 1955 agreement between Ford and the unions stated 'There shall be a National Joint Negotiating Committee which shall consist of not more than one executive official from each of the unions', and went on to say that shop stewards shall be subject to union rules and 'the Agreements arrived at by the National Joint Negotiating Committee'; the 1962 agreement said 'the NJNC calls upon all parties to honour the Agreements'. The disputed 1969 agreement attempted to enforce the words 'honour an agreement' by specifying monetary sanctions ('penal clauses') against those involved in 'unconstitutional action during the six months preceding the start of the period of employment' by loss of pay for lay-offs and short-time working and loss of holiday benefits.

The firm argued that agreements were negotiated on the NJNC by majority votes, and this had not been challenged before. The union lawyers argued (a) there was no agreement, (b) if there was an agreement, it was not intended to be legally binding, and (c) if the agreement was legally binding, the law was being interpreted in a way that Parliament was still debating. The judge found for the unions, and the company had to withdraw the disputed 'penal clauses' before the four week strike was ended. The company estimated its loss at £48 million. The men lost £3 million in wages, and the unions paid £500,000 in strike pay. This overestimates the loss to the men, as large numbers would have drawn social security for their families, which would certainly have come to over double the amount paid out in strike pay. The company would have recovered some of their loss in increased or postponed consumer demand.

The agreement about 'penal clauses' does not seem to have been opposed as a matter of principle. Both the AEF and the T & GWU had signed similar agreements in some parts of engineering and the bus industry. The reaction was triggered off by the resistance of militant workers to a loss of on the spot bargaining power. It also showed the Government that the unions suffered from a lack of effective control over shop stewards and the rank and file. The Government continued to press for the 'In Place of Strife' reforms, as other strikes continued to make the headlines in press, radio and television.

However, there was a mounting wave of protest in the Parliamentary Labour Party against the proposed reforms. There were 132 MPs sponsored by trade unions, and many were under considerable pressure, though direct pressure would have been contrary to Parliamentary procedure. An MP represents a constituency, not a trade union. Nonetheless, the trade unionists in Parliament were probably more aware of the resentment that threats of fines would bring from shop stewards than were those MPs whose lives had by-passed the factory floor.

Mr Wilson insisted that, in the last resort, there must be sanctions against unofficial strikes. He was, however, prepared to negotiate with the TUC; if it would devise its own measures to deal with unofficial strikes, the Government would consider this an alternative to legislation. At a meeting of the Parliamentary Labour Party, Mr Wilson insisted that the Bill on 'industrial relations was essential to economic recovery and full employment. For the Labour Government the passage of this Bill is essential to its continuance in office. There can be no going back on that' (H. Wilson, *op. cit.*, p. 643). Mr Wilson complained later that the last sentence implied that the Government were determined to push through legislation on industrial relations whereas, as he pointed out, there was an offer to the TUC to set its own house in order as a possible alternative. Mrs Castle appeared determined to bring in the Bill, as she was sceptical (rightly as it turned out) of the TUC's ability to settle unofficial strikes. She spoke brilliantly on this topic and won some battles; but like a general without sufficient troops, she lost the campaign.

Lengthy negotiations had taken place between the Government and the TUC. The TUC decided not to change its rules but to give 'a solemn and binding undertaking' to intervene in unofficial strikes. This was probably less than Mr Wilson wanted, as he had asked for a change in Rule 11 of the TUC to deal with unofficial strikes. The ground was allegedly cut from under Mr Wilson's feet by the refusal of the Cabinet to endorse his proposed 'hard line' on the issue. By 18 June, the statement of intent issued by the TUC to the Cabinet said that where a dispute has or will create an important unconstitutional strike, the General Council will assess all the facts, try to arrange a settlement, try to get men back to work within the rules. If the unions did not comply, the General Council would then 'duly report to

Congress or deal with the organisation' as they could do under Rule 13. The Labour Cabinet must have hoped that recalcitrant strikers would be under threat of expulsion, but this did not happen.

Opinions on the 'peacemaking' activities of the TUC vary. Mr Wilson thought that it worked quite well in a period of twelve months before the 1970 Election. The Conservatives and the Press were highly critical. In the event, the TUC had some influence on some strikes, but the numbers of unofficial strikes continued to rise, as they had done steadily since the 1950s with an occasional dip downwards. From 1966 the figures were: 1966–7 1,937; 1967 – 2,116; 1968 – 2,378; 1969 – 3,116; 1970 – 3,906. In the period of the 'solemn and binding undertaking', the number of strikes rose (although it is difficult to measure the strike rate between June 1969 and June 1970, as the figures are measured from January to December by the DEP) by some 20 per cent, while the number of workers on strike rose only 5–6 percent. The number of days lost through strikes, however, rose from 6,925 million in 1969 to 10,908 in 1970. It seemed that workers were staying on strike longer.

The reaction of the Press and the political commentators to the increasing rate of strikes and man-days lost was to give front page treatment to every strike, so that the British public might have been forgiven for thinking that Britain was the most strike-ridden country in the world. Television took over from the newspapers and gave shop stewards an electronic platform (in one large unofficial strike, in which the writer was asked to comment in a television studio, the unofficial strike leaders has been involved in six programmes or interviews in fourteen days, and were exchanging critical comments about the level of fees and the standard of 'hospitality' in each case). Television interviewers were criticised by management for giving excessive coverage to the union's or strikers' case, while the left denounced the 'unfair' treatment of workers by television, saying that incidents were artificially staged and the wildest remarks chosen for presentation. As one shop steward said 'a "punch-up" is news, serious discussion is not'. The nature of the television programme did not make for serious discussion, but for visual impact. Again, management was often reluctant to appear on television and give detailed replies to union or striker criticism. Sometimes their silence was tactical; serious negotiations had to take place, and they did not want to pre-empt the case or negotiate on wages and terms in front of a television audience – though this almost happened on some occasions.

Few journals drew attention to Britain's strike record compared with that of other countries. Table 2 (which shows the man-days lost in industrial disputes) shows the UK to be in fourth place in Western Europe. If the 1968 strike figures for France had been included (they were extremely high and were omitted from the statistics) that country would have been in fourth place and Britain in fifth.

TABLE 2

No. of days lost per 1,000 persons employed

Country	1969	1970	1961–70
Italy	4,110	1,500	1,093
Ireland	2,150	480	1,049
Denmark	70	160	414
UK	520	740	321
France	200	190	306
Belgium	100	870	226
Norway	–	70	115
Netherlands	10	140	25
Germany (West)	20	10	23

If we take Australia, Canada, Japan and the USA for the period 1964–66, we find the days lost per 1,000 employees as follows: Australia 400, Canada 970, Japan 240, USA 870. This gives us some indication of the size of the strike problem, but critics have argued that the short, sharp unofficial British strike is more damaging, economically and politically, than the more formal, longer strikes, with advance warning, of some other industrial countries.

The Conservative Party fought the 1970 General Election on the twin issues of the need to fight rising prices and reduce unemployment ('at a stroke') and to place trade unions within a legal framework, thereby reducing strikes and creating stability in industry. The Conservative Manifesto of May 1970 stated: 'There were more strikes in 1969 than ever before in our history. The rapid and serious deterioration (of our industrial relations) stems directly from Labour's failure to carry through its own policy for the reform of industrial relations'. They promised to establish a 'framework of law within which improved relationships between management, men and unions can develop'.

4 The Industrial Relations Act, 1971

The Industrial Relations Act of 1971, some parts of which became law on 28 February, 1972, has been written about in several articles and books. We propose to consider whether its main aims have been fulfilled. These were to curb unofficial strikes, and in this way strengthen official trade unionism by giving it more power over the militant work groups on the shop floor. This would in turn weaken the force of the lightning strike as a wage lever and slow down the pace and volume of wage demands.

The Conservative Government hoped for great things from the Act. It had a clear mandate from the electorate for its policy of industrial relations reform, with a majority of a hundred or so MPs over the Labour Party. Its intention, forcibly expressed on television and radio, was to curb unofficial strike power, and this was denounced by the left as 'union-bashing'. The Labour Opposition, though it would have been committed, had it been elected, to bringing in a truncated version of 'In Place of Strife', without the fines and penal sanctions, opposed the 1970 Industrial Relations Bill. It is argued that if Parliament had taken more time over the proposed legislation, the first major change in industrial relations for a hundred years, the Act would have been better and acceptance might have been wider. These points were repeatedly made to Mr Carr, Leader of the House, who said that the Bill would have 56 parliamentary days of debate or 481 hours. He objected to the complaints of the Labour Opposition on the lack of time and the use of the 'guillotine to curtail debate as "claptrap"'. 'By any standards, the Bill will have had adequate time for constructive and detailed debate' (House of Commons, 25 August 1971).

The view of the Government was that sufficient time had been given for the debates, but the subsequent development of the Act as law, or non-law, proved them to have underestimated the complexity of the issues. The Bill was not sufficiently examined, though the nature of the debate often obscured the examination of the issues. Reading the Parliamentary Debates, one can form the impression that both sides were more intent on scoring debating points and arguing about the need for more time for debate than they were on ironing out the inadequacies of the Bill. Students of parliamentary debates will be familiar with this point: the Government introduce a Bill which is party policy; the speaking is done by the leading spokesmen of the Government; the backbenchers remain silent, except on the Opposition side, where they speak if they can catch the Speaker's eye; few concessions are made in debate or drafting by the Governments, though the House of Lords may amend some clauses.

The same procedure, or lack of procedure, took place between the Government and the TUC. Since 1945 the custom had been for Governments to consult the TUC on economic, social and industrial relations policies. At times the consultation was more formal than real, particularly on those occasions when the unions were strongly opposed to Government policy. The Industrial Relations Bill was such an occasion, as Mr Carr announced that he was prepared to discuss his Bill with the unions, but the main principles or 'pillars' were not to be altered. These were: the registration of unions, with non-registration leading to loss of legal immunities; the statutory right to join, or not to join, a trade union, along with virtual outlawing of the closed shop; that collective bargaining contracts were presumed to be legally enforceable, unless otherwise stated; that union immunity would be limited in sympathy strikes; that strike ballots and 'cooling-off' periods could be mandatory in 'national emergency' disputes; that some procedure agreements could be statutorily enforced. The trade unions had objected to some of these clauses under the proposed Labour Government Bill; they were bitterly hostile to them under a Conservative government.

While the Government claimed that the Act would strengthen 'responsible trade unionism', critics said that the intention was that the unions should act as 'social policemen' over the industrial conduct of their members. Whether unions would emerge as stronger or weaker depended on the way in which the 'agency shop' (where a registered trade union represents all the employees in an establishment, and all, members or not, contribute to the union or to a charity) or the 'right not to join a union' was interpreted. A trade union was as strong as its power and the will of its members allowed it to be; if in a range of firms or industries numbers of workers insisted on their legal 'right not to join' this could lead either to a weakening of the union or to greater tension or trouble.

One of the main points of the Act was the legal status of collective agreements. As Donovan pointed out, collective agreements in British industry were not intended to be enforceable at law (this was underlined by the decision in the Ford Co. case of 1969). The agreement was now to be legally binding unless there were a written statement to the contrary in the document. The parties to the contract would now be bound to 'use their best endeavours' to maintain industrial peace. Breaches of the agreement would not be settled in courts of law, as is the case with most disputes over contracts, but in a specially extended system of Industrial Tribunals (where a legally qualified chairman would sit with lay members with experience of industrial relation from both sides of industry) and above this a National Industrial Relations

Court (consisting of a president with high legal standing sitting with lay members experienced in industrial relations).

Law has to be supported by sanctions. As the attack was to be on sudden unofficial strikes, these would be treated as a breach of contract. Action would have to be initiated by the employer, or the union if it had a complaint, and application would be to the NIRC. The NIRC might find that industrial relations had been seriously disrupted and refer the case to the Commission on Industrial Relations (CIR). The CIR would then investigate and possibly recommend improved procedures between the parties, mutually agreed where possible, and legally enforceable if the NIRC made an order to this effect.

Given that contracts were legally enforceable between the parties, breaches or infringements could be brought before the Industrial Tribunals (ITs) or NIRC, which would hear the case in a legal manner under Civil Law. Lawyers could represent the union, employer, or parties involved. Witnesses could be required to attend, and documents to be disclosed. As in matrimonial cases, there would be opportunities for conciliation before the case began. The ITs and NIRC could award compensation (to take the most controversial aspect of the new legislation) and this could be enforced through the County Courts. Registered trade unions might still call strikes, although the Secretary of State for Employment could apply for an order stopping or deferring the strike on the grounds of damage to the national economy or security or health, for 60 days. This would be the 'cooling-off' period.

Unfair labour practices were singled out as well as the unofficial strike. These were mainly directed at shop stweards as they referred to threats of strikes against employers to bring in a pre-entry closed shop, or breaches of the agreement, or sympathetic strikes of groups not directly involved in the particular dispute. Strikes to persuade workers to join unions were counted an unfair labour practice.

The situation was summed up by the TUC as follows:

> The Government's attack is aimed primarily at reducing the power of trade unions on the shop floor. It is obviously intended to deal chiefly with what are often referred to as unofficial strikes. Firstly, it sets out through the new system of Registration to control trade union rules, and only gives protection from civil law damages to those who have rules, and only gives protection from civil law damages to those who have authority within those rules. Since unofficial strikers are not formally sanctioned by their trade unions, the leaders of such unofficial strikes could be liable for damages without limit. (*Industrial Relations Bill, Teaching notes for full-time trade union officers* (TUC Education Service, 1970) p. 7).

The Act was long and complicated and one expert has said that 'not one in 100,000 understands it'. (One union official said, in late 1972: 'Most shop stewards know more about Byzantine naval warfare than they do about the I.R. Act'.) We are not concerned here with many of the clauses which relate to other aspects of industrial relations but to the effect on unofficial strikes. No one argues that relations will be better if they are enforced through court action, though the Act's supporters say that legal action should not be necessary and that once the advantages of the legal framework are seen, opposition to the Bill should die down.

Trade union critics pointed to the legal difficulties which would arise and called the legislation a 'Lawyers' Charter'. How, they ask, does one prove in court that a union has used or not used its 'best endeavours' to prevent a strike? Or would the unions now recognise a larger number of disputes as official than they had done before?

How does the law single out those who are inducing workers to break their contract? The public view is of shop stewards haranguing the men to come out on strike, and that such people are clearly responsible for the breach of contract. Yet the Ford shop stewards, who had been on strike for six weeks, claimed in March 1971 that they had to follow the men out, and that the action was a mass one on the men's part. Some trade union leaders have claimed that the new law would need the informer or the 'nark' to tell the authorities who the men were who were inducing a breach of contract.

There was also the charge of unfair labour practices which might involve long legal wrangles. Worse than the decision would be the aftermath, as the employer would presumably be left with a residue of bitterness which might last for some time. Disruptive tactics might also change their shape; besides the strike there were, as Donovan pointed out, a number of actions, such as the go-slow, work-to-rule and overtime ban, which could be just as effective as a withdrawal of labour and could well suit the men better as they involved them in less loss of income.

In the last analysis, said the critics, the law would only be effective if used against individuals or small groups. Any attempt to invoke the law against large numbers of unofficial strikers such as the 6,000 or more at Pilkingtons would simply not work. The classic case of this was the attempt during the war to discipline the unofficial strike of Kent miners (Donovan Report, Appendix 6) which ended in fiasco.

The Industrial Relations Act eventually became law in 1971, in spite of the objections by the trade unions and the TUC (there were peaceful demonstrations, the largest seen in London or other cities for many years, along with two one day strikes by the Engineers and the Transport Workers involving 1 million workers in the first and 2 million in the second). The TUC announced their total opposition to the Act and advised unions not to register, an act which they claimed was not breaking the law but simply non-co-operation, similar to that used by business men who take steps to avoid paying more tax than they are legally required to do. This, they said, was not disobedience but non co-operation, which, if practised on a massive scale, would make the law unworkable. The Government could have taken steps to make this more difficult by altering the law so that all unions were deemed to be registered unless they contracted out, but the unions were sufficiently determined to do this and render themselves liable to huge fines which could have broken them up. It was unlikely that the Government or the average employer would carry the matter to the breaking point, so much depended on a few employers and their determination to enforce the law.

The TUC also advised union officials not to sit on the ITs or NIRC. The CBI criticised this proposed action on the grounds that the unions could have used these courts for pleas of wrongful dismissal and other matters which they wished to pursue, whereas there would be no one on the courts to put the union view. Non co-operation by the unions would make the work of the courts less credible in the eyes of the public. Presumably the Government would invite academics or civil servants to fill the vacant places on such tribunals. While numbers might accept such an invitation, it would not follow, as some MPs and union officials have argued, that such people would be hostile to trade unions. They might take the view that as the Industrial Relations Bill is the law of the land, the best procedure to follow was to see that the judgements of the ITs and NIRC were as fair as possible.

Unfair dismissal

One feature of the Act which was new, was the protection given to the employee against unfair dismissal. This related to the contract of employment and an Industrial Tribunal had to decide whether the dismissal was contractually fair or not. Employees must have 104 weeks continuous employment before they could invoke this particular section. There were a number of clauses relating to fair and unfair dismissal, including the capability and qualifications of the employee, his conduct or whether he was made redundant. The last point brings out an interesting consequence of the Act. Up to 1971, large numbers of employees were arguing before the Industrial Tribunals that they had not been dismissed, they had been made redundant. This enabled them to claim redendancy pay. After the 1971 passage of the Act, the appeal changed sharply: men claimed that they were not redundant, but had been unfairly dismissed. Unlike the eight pillars, this section of the Act was to have some effect.

The machinery of the Act

One of the central purposes of the 1971 Act was the greater importance and powers given to a Chief Registrar and his assistants. There had been a Registrar for many years; indeed, the 1871 Act allowed unions to register, on a voluntary basis, giving them some tax benefits, but this was a clause of no great importance. The new Chief Registrar of 1971 was a far more important figure in the new legislation, and his powers were far-reaching, as were the lists of immunities to trade unions which registered. He could scrutinise union and other organisation rules, to see that members and procedures were dealt with fairly and democratically. Organisations which asked to be placed on the Register must expect a detailed inspection of their rules. Requests for changes in certain rules might be asked for. Failure to comply might, in time, lead to an application to the NIRC to have the registration cancelled or adjourned *sine die*.

The decision of the TUC not to register led to a massive boycott by unions representing millions of workers; this rendered the principle of registration virtually inoperable.

The National Industrial Relations Court (NIRC)

This Court was a new creation of the 1971 Act, and is a Labour Court on the West European or American model. It has the status and powers of a High Court and the Lord Chancellor nominates judges to sit as President of the Industrial Court. The Secretary of State for Employment and the Lord Chancellor appoint other members who have recognised expertise or experience of industrial relations. The original intention was that nominees or people representative of industry and unions would sit to give a wide basis to the Court. The TUC decision not to co-operate with the Act meant it was impossible to appoint any leading union figure. It also seems evident that numbers of academics in the field of industrial relations have been reluctant to sit on the NIRC.

The Court is based in London, but may sit in the provinces. The sitting is usually one judge with possibly two other members, though this may be less or more according to circumstances and consent. Some comment has been made in legal circles about the informality of the NIRC, as there are no red robes or wigs, and the Judge is addressed as 'Mr'. The rules of evidence appear to be more flexible, though there were some protests when the Court said that it might receive some evidence or statements by telephone. But the informality of the NIRC should not conceal its powers. Like other High Courts, it can command the appearance of witnesses and papers, fine and imprison, make interim orders and awards of costs. These awards or fines are enforceable, as the two largest unions in the country, the T & GWU and the AUEW have discovered.

The NIRC is the Court which hears complaints from organisations, or against organisations. Individual cases usually begin with an industrial tribunal. The Court can issue an order of the 'cease and desist' variety, stopping the action which is committing the breach of law; award compensation; or judge on the rights of the dispute. Failure to obey the Court's ruling may lead to any of the above sanctions.

We shall see later how the NIRC works in practice, what its approach has been to the disputes before it, and the remedies or judgements which have resulted.

Industrial tribunals

The above tribunals were not created by the 1971 Act. They had been in existence since the Industrial Training Act of 1964, and they dealt with cases arising from the Contracts of Employment Act of 1963, the Industrial Training Act and the Redundancy Payments Act 1965. Their jurisdiction and scope has been enlarged as each new Act was passed. The area of labour law covered was added to by the Selective Employment Payments Act 1966 and the Equal Pay Act 1970. In a sense these tribunals were the embryo labour courts and, unlike the NIRC, had the support of the TUC and the unions until 1970. The Ministry of Labour said in its evidence to the Donovan Commission that the work of industrial tribunals could be expanded, although the TUC argued that the tribunals should concern themselves mainly with employment problems and leave the interpretation of collective agreements to normal negotiations between unions and employers.

The tribunals have a legal chairman flanked by two wingmen drawn from panels agreed by employers and unions. They sit in regional centres throughout Britain and act as a fairly speedy channel for claims from industrial workers. Most of these claims arose from the Redundancy Payments Act 1965, and the total amount paid out was far greater than the estimates the Government had made; £25 million was paid out in 1966 (the year when unemployment rose sharply at the end), £50 million in 1967, £62 million in 1969. This created much work for the tribunals (K. W. Wedderburn *The Worker and the Law* 2nd ed., Penguin, 1971, pp. 126–127). Wedderburn points out that the Minister of Labour intended in 1965 that the tribunals would be 'easy of access... speedy... with less formality and expense' than the normal courts. If this were the Minister's intention he cannot have sat in many tribunals or many courts, as the former are more formal than most magistrates' courts.

On the existing, but expanded, system of tribunals the 1971 Act superimposed two main new tasks of interpretation: the sections relating to unfair dismissal, and those relating to the rights which workers have under the Act, such as complaints against employers and the other designated unfair industrial practices. Cases can be appealed from the tribunals to the NIRC. We shall see later that, although the TUC boycott of the Act has almost denuded the tribunals of official trade union representation, several important cases relating to unfair dismissal have had their effect on the employer-employee relationship, and also on union negotiations with employers. As the Act allows individuals to bring grievances or cases before the tribunals, there have been a number of decisions and we shall deal with these later.

The Commission on Industrial Relations (CIR)

There is a close relationship between the industrial tribunals and the NIRC, and they are part of the legal machinery buttressing the Act. The CIR existed before 1971, as it was set up as a voluntary agency in 1969, but it became a statutory body in 1971. Its role is seen as an advisory body, which will undertake research and inquiry into industrial relations, with a view to publishing proposals for improvements. The CIR will also have powers to command witnesses and documents, and refusal to co-operate may lead to a fine of £100; it has not used this power, preferring to work by consent. It can supervise the ballots for the agency shop, supply names and addresses for ballots under the special procedures (as they did during the Rail ballot of 1972), and also deal with references on industrial relations sent to it by the Secretary of State or the Government.

The relationship between the CIR and the NIRC is partly covered above, with the need for ballots under the Act, whether agency shop, special procedure, or sole bargaining agent. Its main approach is directed to the improvement of collective bargaining and procedures; this includes recognition and representational rights, and the abolition of wages councils when collective bargaining in hitherto weakly organised industries has improved. The CIR will carry out enquiries for the NIRC and make recommendations.

The CIR has done considerable work on defining bargaining agents in some industries, and on general topics such as the role of employers' organisations in industrial relations. The fundamental message here, easier to state than to achieve, is:

National and domestic bargaining need not be in conflict but should be complementary. The achievement of a correct balance between different bargaining levels is neither an easy nor a once-and-for-all process, but it is one which is essential for the reform of wages structure in the United Kingdom. (Employers Organisations and Industrial Relations, HMSO, December 1972).

This approach is complemented by the CIR's study of disclosure of information to trade union representatives to assist in negotiation and make for good industrial relations.

The Code of Industrial Relations

The preamble to the Industrial Relations Act laid down the four principles of free collective bargaining, orderly procedures for the settlement of disputes, free associations for workers and employers, and freedom from unfair treatment for workers. While the Act develops the legal background of these proposals in detail, the Secretary of State has a duty to produce, and keep up to date, a code giving guidance to industry on the application of these principles. This has been compared to the Highway Code, though it is to be hoped that the Industrial Code will have more influence on behaviour and attidues in industry than the Highway Code has on the habits of drivers. The Code is advisory, not statutory, although it will be admissable as evidence in court actions, and can influence legal judgements where relevant.

The Code (Industrial Relations, Code of Practice)was published in June 1971 and became law in February 1972, and makes a number of general statements about the need for better industrial relations, for which management must take most responsibility. Its intention is 'to give practical guidance for promoting good industrial relations'. The two main themes are 'reasonable and constructive' collective bargaining, for which strong unions are needed; and good human relations, 'based on trust and confidence'. Management are urged to negotiate, consult and communicate with recognised unions, which they are asked to welcome. Machinery has to be devised for better negotiations. Trade unions are exhorted to maintain joint arrangements for negotiations and consultation, to train their shop stewards, and encourage member participation. Employers' associations are asked to co-operate in the above proposals, and to collect, analyse, advise and circulate information about industrial relations to their members. Industrial employees are reminded of their obligations and their rights. They are asked to be aware of their contract of employment, and of their collective bargaining agreements.

Suggestions are made about manpower and employment policies, recruitment, selection, training, pay systems, status and security, and working conditions. Much of what this section has to say is admirable, though good employers have done thus for years, and backward employers may ignore its suggestions. The difficulties arise over interpretation. For instance, in December 1972, the British Steel Corporation had to announce large scale closures and redundancies. Although their industrial relations department is progressive and humane, the steelworkers affected protested vigorously. How does this square with the Code's 'avoid unnecessary fluctuations in manpower, where changes are necessary, make them with as little disruption as is practicable to the employee concerned'?

Consultation and communication are said to be essential. Employees, supervisors, managers and unions should be kept informed, by speech and training, by written information and meetings. Employees should have statutory information about terms and conditions, rules and procedures, as well as other relevant information. Consultation on a formal basis should take place in establishments with over 250 employees. This should give opportunities to exchange views and information. The joint committee should have a constitution and report back to constituents. Consultation should be encouraged in all sizes of establishments, so as to find 'mutually acceptable solutions' through 'a genuine exchange of views'.

The above is buttressed and enlarged by the section on 'Employee Representation at the Place of Work'. This defines the role and responsibilities, the appointment and qualifications, status, facilities for and training of shop stewards, along with the grievance and disputes procedures, individual and collective, which are suggested.

Comments on the above two sections must be that good firms already do as suggested, but that there is a wide area of wasteland, especially in the field of consultative committees. Where such committees do exist, they are felt by workers to be ineffective, as they have little influence on important decisions. The Code does not discuss the relationship between the consultative committees and the shop stewards, or the union. It is to be hoped that management will pay some attention to the suggestions on training, as some firms, even nationalised industries, are still unwilling to co-operate in releasing shop stewards with pay, for day release courses. A CIR report, 'Industrial Relations Training', of December 1972, states that in 1970 'only 20 per cent of managers... and 15 per cent of shop stewards attended courses which included industrial relations'. These amounted to one day or less for 'half the managers and one-third of the shop stewards'. In the majority of establishments surveyed no industrial relations courses had been attended. Reports of this nature expose the weaknesses behind the good intentions of the Code, though they point out the remedies if industry and government will make and seize the opportunities.

50

The section on 'Collective Bargaining' is the most important part of the Code. Its implementation would change the present system dramatically. The Code follows the IR Act in seeking to end fragmented collective bargaining, with bargaining units covering as large a number of employees with common interest as possible. A number of definitions of bargaining units include: work, training, organisation of work, payment systems, professional and other qualifications. Claims for the recognition of unions include the above, as well as the numbers of members, though not their identity. Disputes between rival unions can eventually be referred to the TUC's Bridlington Agreement; ballots under the Act to the CIR.

Once negotiations between management and unions are established, collective agreements should be developed and extended through regular joint meetings. Procedural and substantive rules should be defined. The former deals with union recognition, constitution, terms and procedures for settlement of disputes, job security and discipline. The latter includes wages, hours of work, holidays and other terms and conditions of employment. More information should be provided by management, unless this might help a competitor, to assist responsible negotiations. This may mean less than some unions hoped for, as the minimum is the information supplied annually to shareholders.

A development of collective bargaining on these lines would lend great formality to the British contract, as well as extending its scope more in the direction of the US pattern. A separation of the procedural and substantive issues, if done properly, might reduce the number of strikes, as the US unions go to arbitration on procedural issues. In Britain disputes arise over the procedural as well as the substantive issues as there is little attempt to separate them. The distinction is also made in parts of Western Europe over disputes of right (procedural) and disputes of interest (substantive). Agreements should be in writing.

It was the hope of Mr Carr that the Code would provide a check list for action, and stimulate companies to review their policies. Unions would also be able to use the Code as a bargaining lever against management in order to raise issues. While some use is being made of the Code in negotiations by unions, the union opposition to the Act may have led to less written agreements rather than more. Nearly all major companies agreed with unions that the first clause of the agreement would state 'Nothing in this agreement shall be enforceable at law'.

The TUC published 'Good Industrial Relations: A Guide for Negotiators' in November 1971. In many of its points there is some affinity with the Code, but the 29 pages do not mention the existence of the Act or the Code. This is deliberate, as the opening sentence points out 'The only effective method of conducting industrial relations in an industrialised and democratic society is through voluntary collective bargaining leading to agreements between trade unions and employers'. (p. 5, 3rd reprint, July 1972).

Collective bargaining is said to be a joint activity, in which divergent interests emerge. Rules are needed to contain and channel conflict. Managers no longer have 'unchallenged prerogatives' and work-people need to agree on many decisions which may affect them. 'Widening the range of issues on which negotiations take place, and making the procedures more speedy and equitable, will go a considerable way towards improving industrial relations' (p. 7).

As might be expected, the TUC goes into greater detail on the scope of agreements, wages and salaries, than the Code does. Other differences concern the principle of the 'status quo', which is explained as follows:

'It is agreed that in the event of any difference arising which cannot immediately be disposed of, then whatever practice or agreement existed prior to the difference shall continue to operate pending a settlement or until the agreed procedure has been exhausted' (p. 15).

The disclosure of information by employers and firms referred to in the Code is spelt out in considerable detail by the TUC. The information asked for here is much more than most firms possess at the present time, and goes further than the CIR report 'Disclosure of Information'.

Another difference of opinions comes with the question of trade union membership, defined as the objective of 100 per cent membership. Conscientious objections to trade unionism are recognised 'But the majority of non-unionists have no such conscientious objections, their actions merely serve to undermine the collective strength of their fellows' (p. 21).

Though there is much agreement on a wide range of issues in industrial relations between the Code and the TUC 'Guide', there is no doubt that the Code operates within a legal framework, whereas the TUC insists on voluntary collective negotiations and collective rights of workers having priority over individual rights of workers.

TUC reaction to the proposals

The TUC mobilised its forces against the Industrial Relations Bill at an early stage. By March 1971 it had called a special conference at Croydon. Large numbers of demonstrators gathered outside the hall in the rain. The General Council said it was totally opposed to the Bill as it endangered the orderly development of industrial relations. The effects of strikes had been exaggerated: with 11 million working days lost in 1970, this only meant a half day lost per worker per year. Legal proceedings would create and prolong strikes. 'We have sought, and will continue, to prevent the Bill reaching the Statute Book'.

Mr Feather argued that the Government did not understand the strength of feeling. The Bill was about the balance of power between employers and unions. The TUC objectives were: 1) to create a movement of resistance; 2) to explain the Bill to the public. The Government had attempted to push the Bill through quietly, and the Labour Opposition could only debate about one in three of the 150 clauses due to the time limit and the guillotine imposed. The TUC could choose whether it accepted a *fait accompli* and co-operated to make the law work and protect members, or practised total opposition to a repugnant Bill, in which event the TUC could vote to assist members who defy the law. The TUC's own suggestion was to steer a middle course by non co-operation. Members should not break the law even though the Government was bringing the law into disrepute. Unions should not assist the Industrial Relations Bill in any way, and oppose it by all legal means. The Labour Party should announce their intention of repealing the Act at the first opportunity. Unions should not register or accept if placed on the register. There were financial risks in non-registration, but principles were at stake. One day stoppages and strikes would not prevent the passage of the Bill.

Some union officials called for strikes against the Bill but others, chiefly white-collar unions like NALGO and NUT, said this would be irresponsible. Mr Chapple of the Electrical, Electronics and Plumbing Trade Union (EEPTU) swam against the tide of the Conference. He agreed that the Bill was so ill-defined that the Government could not predict what its effects would be, then suggested that the TUC might ask the Government to withdraw the legislation and guarantee one strike-free year. This brought boos and a slow handclap.

The TUC agreed to support non-registration and non co-operation arguments about the Industrial Relations Bill.

Most newspapers took the view that some legal framework was necessary to help prevent unofficial strikes and this turned out to be the major issue. Of the many debates which took place, in Parliament and on television and radio, the argument came to be between the voluntaristic and the legalistic schools of union reform. The first group used the Donovan Report as their bible; the second argued that voluntarism would not stop the wildcat strike and that unions should be given remedies against their unofficial strikers. The binding collective contract would be the means of enforcing this. This was the argument deployed by those who said that the Bill would strengthen unions, not weaken them. The Bill would also remove grievances by giving workers the chance to appeal against unfair dismissal, the right to form and to join trade unions, all of which had caused strikes in the past.

The voluntaristic group argued that the right to join a trade union was a social right, whereas the right not to join was an individual one. The two raised an unnecessary conflict, and would be resented by unionists. The closed shop was a group right, whereas the Government stress on the freedom of the individual worker was aimed at weakening the unions.

Advocates of the Bill said that labour legislation was usually opposed by labour in most countries. In the USA the Taft Hartley Act of 1947 (on which the IR Bill was modelled), was denounced by the American unions as the 'slave labour' Act, but they now worked with it. Yet even some supporters of the Bill were doubtful about the benefits of law and the courts, as industrial relations were best left to negotiation and accommodation. They were doubtful if it were wise to rely on unions to discipline members. As subsequent events were to show, the weak points in the IR Act were the difficulties of solving industrial disputes by turning to the courts, and the unwillingness or inability of unions to control illegally striking members. Finally, the supporters of the Bill did not appear to have tested the temperature of industrial support. In many industries, a strike might be ten or twenty times as expensive for the company as the granting of a pay rise would be. Even if there were no strikes bad industrial relations and bad publicity might be worse for a firm. As events proved, the majority of British companies did not wish to court labour trouble by using the IR Act.

The Government claimed that the Bill was 'history in the making'. It insisted that the law would not be draconian, and that standards would be laid down for good industrial relations, which would have an influence, like the Highway Code, and help to develop better procedures. The legal enforcement of contracts would make people more careful of breaking them. The effect of registration would be to increase trade union control over members through the rule-book. There would be no protection for anyone who was not an official of a registered union. Unions would thereby be strengthened, not weakened. Taken at its lowest point, the Bill was an attempt to do something about an industrial relations system in disrepute. As for union objections, refusal to register and to nominate for, or sit on, the industrial tribunals and NIRC, this opposition would disappear in a year or so.

Against this, the critics argued that the four years since Donovan had been wasted in barren conflict over the legal enforcement of contract, and that the changes were so fundamental that the majority of unions would oppose them for years. This forecast was reinforced by the determination of the new Conservative Government of 1970 to be 'firmer' or 'more abrasive' in its dealings with the unions than was its Labour predecessor. The General Election had been fought partly on the issue of rising prices, linked to trade union pressure for wage increases and backed by the threat of unofficial strike action, and partly by the 'law and order' issue, in which student riots, anti-apartheid demonstrations and militant shop stewards were all made to appear in the public eye as one red-eyed group of troublemakers.

5 Law and Labour Relations in Other Countries

In most western industrialised countries the unions find themselves under some legal regulation. The 'right to strike' is written into some constitutions as a civic freedom, while in others the right to strike is implicit as a democratic right rather than as an explicit promise. This is in contrast to the position in two thirds of the world, where the unions are favoured in theory, as in the Communist countries, yet never officially strike. The Communists find no difficulty in explaining this apparent paradox. 'Communism', they say, 'means that the workers have taken over the State. The State and its properties are now owned by the workers. A strike is, by definition, a strike against workers as a whole, and would be meaningless'. In spite of this, strikes have taken place in some Communist countries.

In military states of the South American, African or Asian variety, strikes are discouraged if not outlawed, as harmful to the nation. There are laws against strikes which can be enforced, as in the Communist states, by strong police or military action.

Democratic countries in the West still pay lip service to the freedom to strike, but many have passed regulations which make it extremely difficult to do so, especially for those who are not well organised, or are not working through trade union collective contracts. In the West German Works Constitution Act of January 1972 it states 'Acts of industrial warfare between the employer and the works council shall be unlawful; the foregoing shall not apply to industrial disputes between collective bargaining parties' (Sec. 74 (2)). Other countries, such as Holland and Belgium, have agreements which contain an industrial peace clause. In Holland this may be enforced at civil law, but this is seldom done. Belgium stipulates in the National Agreement on Social Planning (1964) that 'the parties will refrain from all hostile acts towards one another during the period stipulated for negotiations'. Failure to agree after a period leaves the parties free to use industrial or other action. 'No-strike' clauses are beginning to be more common in Italy, though the strike problem there is the large scale, but short, political strike.

West European attitudes to the closed shop vary from those in Britain, where 'closed shops' are to be found in a number of industries, despite the Industrial Relations Act. West European unions are split on religious and political grounds between Christian, Socialist and Communist unions. For these reasons a closed shop would be more discriminatory than in Britain, with its homogeneous union movement, and it is usually forbidden unless exercised against the non-unionist.

Comparisons of labour law in different countries may be difficult. The legal concepts can be translated and understood by lawyers but their operation often takes place in a different culture, with different attitudes to labour law. The German system varies on three different levels: the individual contract of employment, the workshop situation, and the collective bargaining contract, usually at a national level. The individual contract gives the employee status, rights and duties; work and performance may be specified at length, and there are obligations not to do faulty work and, not to persuade another worker to breach his contract, though he can join in a legal strike. He has to respect certain rules of secrecy relating to his employer's business. The employer's obligations are lengthy and specific, relating to wages, welfare, job security, holidays, pensions and dismissal.

The German Works Council Act, 1972, has already been noted. Works councils exist by statute in most firms, meet at least once a month, and can deal with personnel, social and economic matters. The most far-reaching aspect of the past Works Constitution Acts was the creation of worker representation at the level of company management, or worker directors. This began in the coal and steel industries. Where co-determination exists, the employer must negotiate with his works council on such matters as hours of work, incentive schemes and certain related issues which may be taken to compulsory arbitration. Breaches of works rules may be dealt with by works courts made up of equal numbers of employees and management. Reprimands and warnings can be given, and small fines, paid usually to a charity or community fund.

Disputes in collective bargaining are divided between disputes over interests and disputes over rights. Interests are defined as the basic material of collective bargaining, whereas rights are the legal aspect of the contract. The legal aspect can be put to compulsory arbitration.

Provision is made under German law for conciliation, mediation and arbitration. Labour ministries in the various Länder (regions) appoint a suitably qualified person to bring consenting parties to the dispute together. Arbitration commissions are also set up, with equal representation from employers and labour. The arbitration award is binding. Numbers of agreements mention conciliation and the procedures for settling disputes. While numbers of British agreements make the same point, the distinction is that in Germany the agreement can be enforced with some success; for instance, the 1964 agreement in metalworking between the union (I.G. Metall) and the employer provides for a cooling off period of up to 22 days, during which the mediation procedures must be exhausted and no strikes or lockouts may take place... fines (may be) as high as 1 million DM (£100,000)' (Seyforth,

Shaw *Labour Relations and the Law,* University of Michigan, 1969, p. 137).

One important difference between the German and British systems is that, in the former, grievances and complaints are usually put to the works council by the employee, instead of through the shop steward, as is the case in Britain. This removes a number of issues from work-place argument, and seems to be one reason for the much lower incidence of disputes and days lost in Germany. Works council members are given more time and scope to deal with complaints than are shop stewards, although the situation in now changing due to the 1972 Works Constitution Act.

Sweden has long recognised the enforceability of the collective agreement. The custom of drawing up agreements based on reciprocal rights and obligations began in industry during the nineteenth century, and a Supreme Court judgement in 1915 held that the agreement was a contract in law. Swedish employers appeared to be content that the principle was established; there was little attempt to enforce collective agreements at law, for two reasons: firstly, the long delays of the legal process in a civil action; secondly, the reluctance to let the law judge the merits of industrial relations disputes. In 1928 a legal framework for industrial relations was provided through the Labour Court Act and the Act on Collective Agreements. The gist of these Acts is contained in the statement: 'The rule of law demanded that the solution of disputes concerning collective agreements should not depend upon the respective powers of the belligerent parties' (Folke Schmidt, 'Settlement of Employment Grievances/in Sweden' in B. Aaron (ed.) *Labour Courts and Grievance Settlement in Western Europe,* University of California Press, 1971, p. 167). Although the Swedish labour movement objected to this law at the time, and protests were organised, the Acts were soon accepted. This acceptance stemmed from the victory of the Social Democrats soon after the Acts, and the policy of full employment and rising living standards which followed.

For many years after 1945, Sweden was seen as an example of a model industrial relations system. There was an incomes policy, agreed between the employers' associations and the unions, of a highly centralised nature. Stress was put on equitable wages and the parties kept the pay/price spiral within bounds. Foreign visitors, especially from Britain, returned home impressed and wrote appreciative accounts of the self discipline and social justice of the system. A wave of strikes in 1970, involving many workers in the public sector, destroyed this image. Although unofficial strikes are illegal under the Basic Agreement, and the duty to negotiate in good faith is also a legal requirement, both requirements are breached from time to time, especially in the building industry. Most unofficial strikes are not taken to the Labour Court, but one study showed four cases out of thirteen taken there.

The statutory maximum fine is 200 Sw.Kr., or two days pay, which is hardly a deterrent.

Labour law in the USA

As much of the British Industrial Relations Act was borrowed or taken from the labour law of the United States, it is worth looking at the body from which the organs for the transplant were taken. The main body of modern law was developed in the 1930s and 1940s, partly as a reaction to the Great Depression which dented public confidence in free enterprise business and led to 15 million unemployed.

The union movement was at a low ebb, with less than 3 million members, mostly in craft-type unions. The mass production industries were almost unorganised. Unions objected to company unionism (unions organised or controlled by employees in the pay of employers and possessing little real independence from management). Company unions were reinforced by the 'yellow dog' contract, in which workers had to promise, as a condition of employment, not to engage in certain union activities such as collective bargaining or striking. Unions were threatened by the use of the injunction, which restrained them from breaching 'yellow dog' contracts. The injunction also gave some judges the chance to exercise anti-union opinions, as well as leading to the possibility of fines or imprisonment.

Congress passed the Norris-La Guardia Act in 1932, removed the stigma of conspiracy in law from unions, and gave them the right to bargain collectively with employers. The use of the injunction in labour disputes was to be discouraged. Next year came the National Industrial Recovery Act (Wagner Act), which affirmed the unions' right to bargain collectively and also to organise through representatives of their own choosing and without hindrance, restraint or coercion on the part of employers. The National Labor Relations Board was set up to supervise elections in plants where employees wanted to form or choose a union. The NLRB also had some influence on the type of union, whether craft or industrial. The 1930s saw a dramatic increase in trade union membership, due partly to the economic recovery and partly to the stimulus provided by the Wagner Act, which defined anti-union employer practices as 'unfair'. In 1933 only 5.6 per cent of the labour force was unionised; by 1939 it had risen to 16.7 per cent and, by 1945, 26.1 per cent. Since then the percentage has dropped slightly.

The 1930s has been called the decade of labour, but the growing strength of the unions and the great increase in strikes (partly because of the development of the Congress of Industrial Organisation (CIO), which set up as a rival union movement in the mass production industries to the American

58

Federation of Labour), especially the wartime strikes of coal miners led by John L. Lewis, led to demands for legal curbs on trade union power. The large number of strikes immediately after 1945, and the accusations against some unions of racketeering, coincided with a Republican Congress, which passed the Taft-Hartley Act in 1947. The Act is said to have swung the balance of power from labour towards business. 'Unfair employer practices' are offset by the recognition of 'unfair labour practices' on the part of unions.

Those who advocated the introduction of Taft-Hartley type law to Britain should have noted that the first section of US labour law, the Wagner Act, was welcomed by the unions. It gave them a chance to organise freely, it removed the threat of legal action and led, after a period of organising, to the development of the comprehensive collective bargaining contract. Whereas British unions have been suspicious of the written contract, US unions have demanded it, and contracts there can contain a hundred or so pages.

Terms of the Contract

The purpose of the contract has been defined by the US Bureau of Labour Statistics as

> an expression of the various rights, duties, and privileges which a union and an employer have agreed shall be in effect for a specified period of time ... [it] is to define the status of the workers organisation, to specify the terms and conditions of employment, and to set forth the plan for adjusting grievances and disputes that may arise during the life of the agreement itself' (US Bureau of Labor Statistics, *Bulletin* no. 686, Washington, DC 1942, p. 1).

The many topics which can be included in the contract include purpose of contract, length and duration of the agreement, renewal or extension, union status and wage provisions (this covers many of the aspects of wages such as incentive plans, wage adjustments and time studies; overtime, shift work, Sunday and holiday work and vacations are naturally included). One group which may seem unusual to British observers is that covering seniority, lay-off and re-employment, promotion, transfers, and so on. Provisions are made in a formal manner for grievance procedure, strikes and lockouts; this is a standard feature of contracts and stands in sharp distinction to British practice. A typical clause may run: 'It is agreed that the union will not call a strike and the employer will not institute a lockout for any cause whatsoever during the term of the agreement' (*ibid.* p. 162).

As union-management relations have become more formalised, so new factors enter into the contract, clauses proliferate and lawyers are needed to interpret the agreements. At the same time, the contracts are not uniform in length or contents. A study of the prevalence of certain contract provisions shows that only one tenth of agreements allowed for employer payments to workers losing time, or being called up, either to the Armed Forced or allied organisations. (See US Department of Labor *Bulletin* no. 1181, 'Labor-Management Contract Provisions', 1954, p. 1.)

Management has become increasingly concerned with the expansion of union power into the realm of managerial authority: hiring, dismissal, promotion, transfer, lay-offs, discipline, wages and production. The defence against the union encroachment on the management's preserve has taken one form, that of drawing the boundaries between union and management territory with the legal precision of an international commission, or perhaps two rival powers agreeing on spheres of influence. The agreement between the Illinois division of the Service Pipe Line Company (part of a pipe line which stretches from the Great Lakes to the Gulf of Mexico) and the Oil Workers International Union (CIO) contains the following clause, article 35: 'It is understood and agreed that the rights which the Company had prior to the signing of this agreement are retained by the Company except those specifically abridged, delegated, granted or modified by this agreement' (May 1952). The agreement between Local Union 501, UAW-CIO and the Bell Aircraft Corporation, contains 4 clauses, 12, 13, 14 and 15, on managerial prerogatives:

> The Company shall exercise the usual functions, duties and responsibilities of Management without interference or hindrance by the Union, except as abridged by the terms of this agreement.
>
> The Company has the complete and sole right to determine the extent of its operations. It shall determine when any part of the complete operation shall function or be halted, and when production shall be increased or decreased.

The other two clauses deal with hiring, discipline, dismissal and promotion.

The problem of drawing the lines of management influence is not solved by inserting clauses in a contract. The right of management to manage all aspects of production and the right of the union to organise, secure the best conditions for its members, and protect them by controlling jobs and work speeds is bound to conflict increasingly with management functions. Disputes frequently arise in spite of a 'no-strike' clause in most contracts, but these disputes are usually settled by arbitration. Many of the arbitration clauses in contracts were introduced in wartime by the War Labor Board. Although unofficial strikes did take place, a gradual acceptance of arbitration developed, and many disputes are settled either by private arbitration, or by the NLRB. This procedure defuses many of the situations which, in Britain, lead to shop stewards calling an unofficial strike. If men are disciplined or dismissed in the USA, the union usually notes this and brings the issue to arbitration. Disputes over wage increases usually take place towards the end of the annual, or two-year, contract. The resulting strike may be large scale, but it is official and predictable, and causes less disruption to industry than does the British 'lightning' strike. Collective agreements in the USA are enforceable by law, and damages can be given against unions for breach of contract. In practice this is seldom done, for the reasons also given by British business, that the legal process takes too long and the bitterness may last.

The chief differences between the US and the British system lie in the comprehensiveness of the American contract, the separation of disputes between those arising out of the negotiation of the contract, and those which come during the period of the contract. Added to this is the practice of 'one union, one plant', or the support of labour law for one union having jurisdiction over a particular bargaining unit. The latter practice reduces the number of inter-union disputes over which union claims which workers, and jurisdictional disputes over 'who does what'. US labour law, particularly the influence of the NLRB, has led to a widespread acceptance of 'one plant, one union'. This had led to the greater formalisation of US procedures and much more work for labour lawyers. But unions and management avoid using the criminal or civil law, and settle their differences through a local and speedy process of arbitration.

There are more days lost through strikes per worker in the US than in Britain. Most of this is due to the large set-piece strike at the end of the contract, which may be for one, two or three years. There is less disruption during the life of the contract, due to the 'no-strike' clause and the acceptance of arbitration.

But the US has found that the legal enforcement of the collective contract through court action does not work. State and municipal employees are forbidden by law to strike, yet there has been large scale union growth in these areas and the authorities have been powerless to prevent strike action. Injunctions have been issued by courts against groups as varied as subway employees, dustmen, policemen, teachers and hospital workers, and arrests and imprisonment has been carried out. This has proved ineffective as the strikes continued, while those leaders who have been imprisoned emerged from jail with their union leadership greatly strengthened by their temporary martyrdom. Where such public strikes were prevented by legal threats, workers have found ways round and through the law by work-to-rules, go-slows and more American variants such as the 'blue flue' (thousands of police report sick with 'flu on the same day) or 'go-quick' (police charge every motorist breaking the law and the court system is overloaded and the authorities besieged by angry motorists).

The US system of labour law has no universal legal panacea. The chief aspects of the system that could be welcomed here would be: the greater formalisation and scope of the collective contract; a reduction in the number of unions in plants; and the acceptance of independent arbitration for the speedy settlement of disputes.

Arbitration in the USA

There are three main bodies of arbitrators in the USA: The American Arbitration Association, the National Academy of Arbitrators, and the Federal Mediation and Conciliation Service (USFC & MS). The latter body is a Government agency and arises from the Labor Management Relations Act of 1947. The 1969 Report states that more mediators were required than at any time in the history of the Service. In five out of six cases handled by mediators, a settlement was reached without a work stoppage. The increasing extent of arbitration can be seen from the Table 3.

TABLE 3

Arbitration Unit Workload

	1969	1968	1967	1966	1965	1964	1963	1962	1961	1960
Awards	2640	2309	1967	2441	1887	1952	1618	1733	1553	1320

Arbitration is encouraged by the US Labor Relations law. The USFM & CS seeks to reach an agreement between the parties to a dispute. Failing this, they may submit 'to the employees in the bargaining unit ... the employer's last offer of settlement for approval or rejection in a secret ballot'. This is not done often, as the workers usually vote in support of their union leaders' demands. One of the chief features of the 1947 Act is the 'duty to bargain collectively' which means that the contract cannot be breached during its life unless there is sixty days notice prior to the expiry date. The USFM & CS has to be notified within thirty days of the existence of a dispute, when it may deploy its various powers and services.

There is wide compliance with the law regarding the thirty days notice: in 1969, 80,353 such notices were received by the USFM & CS. The majority of the disputes were settled by normal collective bargaining, though some 8,000 required joint or separate mediation conferences and another 10,936 required informal mediation. Work stoppages occurred in 15 per cent of the cases closed by mediation.

Some patience is required by the parties to the dispute. Though the USFM & CS attempts to deal with disputes as speedily as possible, some delay is inevitable. The following analysis of a sample 643 arbitration cases shows that the average *per diem* rate for arbitrations was around the $150 mark, much less than lawyers would charge in Britain when we remember that the average US salary is three times as high as in Britain. The procedure followed shows the sequence: grievance filed and request for panel – 80 days; list sent – 3 days; time between date list sent and appointment – 32 days; time between appointment and hearing – 61 days; time between hearing and award – 49 days. The total time between the request for arbitration and the award is around 150 days. A British system based on this would have to function more quickly, which should be possible. It would be necessary to operate with speed as some shop stewards think there is no difficulty which a short sharp strike cannot cure. As long as such strikes achieve their object there is little future for arbitration, which requires the confidence and patience of employers and unions.

Costs of arbitration in the USA are reasonable. They would be less still if the legal fees were excluded. These amount to two and a half times the arbitration fee. The USFM & CS urges arbitrators not to raise their fees over $150 daily, as they want the service to be widely available. Most arbitrators seem to conform to this.

One difficulty facing the USFM & CS is rather like the British airlines' difficulty with training young pilots and then asking senior pilots and passengers to accept them as fully competent to fly planes. Lists of arbitrators are sent to the parties, who tend to select the experienced, so that a small percentage do the great majority of cases.

There are demands that the delays in US arbitration should be ended, as well as that the process should be improved in other ways. One arbitrator suggests better and earlier investigation of grievances, greater willingness to throw out grievances without merit, better preparation for cases, improved presentation of cases, more precise contract language, less delay from the filing of the grievance to the hearing, less 'excessive' arbitration arising from the earlier points, better performance by the arbitrator, less wordiness in writing, simpler courtroom aids, more new faces, less institutionalisation of procedures, and stress on the judicial process rather than conflict. The writer calls this his 'dirty dozen' of complaints, but argues that arbitration is by far the best approach in industrial relations for disputes, providing the process is speedy and the results are mutually binding. (See Harold W. Davey, 'Arbitration as a Substitute for Other Legal Remedies' *Labor Law Journal*, October 1972, p. 595).

6 The Eight Pillars of the Act

The Act itself was introduced with the intention of amending the law relating to industrial relations; establishing a National Industrial Relations Court; widening the scope of the existing industrial tribunals; appointing a Chief Registrar of Trade Unions and Employers Associations and his assistants; and to establishing a Commission on Industrial Relations as a statutory body. The Act develops these proposals in detail, but introduces them along with its general principles:

(a) the principle of collective bargaining freely conducted on behalf of workers and employers and with due regard to the general interests of the community;

(b) the principle of developing and maintaining orderly procedures in industry for the peaceful and expeditious settlement of disputes by negotiation, conciliation or arbitration, with due regard to the general interests of the community;

(c) the principle of free association of workers in independent trade unions, and of employers in employers' associations, so organised as to be representative, responsible and effective bodies for regulating relations between employers and workers; and,

(d) the principle of freedom and security for workers, protected by adequate safeguards against unfair industrial practices, whether on the part of employers or others.

The principles appear to be unexceptionable, but closer examination shows the phrase 'the general interests of the community' in both (a) and (b). This is another phrase for 'the national interest' and the unions view this critically: 'Unions and workpeople have learned from experience that when the cry "The National Interest" goes up, it means everybody but them. The Government seems to think that the national interest and the interest of the employers is one and the same thing' (TUC *Reason: the case against the Government's proposals on Industrial Relations*, London 1971). The unions appear correct in their interpretation: community interests are interpreted by the Government, and the government of the day makes a political decision about them. Collective bargaining is no longer left to unions and employers, as the State has a third party interest on behalf of the community. The second principle appears to relate to the enforceability of agreements; the third to the right to form unions (this is a new right), but also deals with the conduct of unions;

the fourth raises the question of the closed shop and compulsory unionism.

Mr Carr said he was prepared to discuss the Bill with the unions, but the central features of the new law, or the 'eight pillars' must stand. The first of these is *registration*. While registration of unions had been in existence for one hundred years, it was voluntary and did not make much difference to the conduct of unions; now registration was to have 'teeth' and the Chief Registrar would scrutinise the rules of unions and their contents. The unions saw this as a device to query the power of shop stewards over members, who could not be 'excluded from membership... by way of any arbitrary or unreasonable discrimination'. (Sec. 65 (b)). We shall see this section later in the dispute between the AUEW and Mr Goad. Members must have full rights to nominate, contest and hold office. These rights were already held by paid-up members, conditional on length of membership in the case of holding office. More importantly, members would not face 'unfair or unreasonable disciplinary action' in their refusing to take part of strikes or 'irregular industrial action short of a strike'. If a member did face such action, he must have full and proper notice, a fair hearing and a written statement. Members must not be restricted by union rules from using courts or tribunals.

The Registrar would have the power to use sanctions against unions whose rules he did not approve. If unapproved rules were not altered, the Registrar could apply to the Industrial Court for a cancellation of the union's registration. He would also have the power to examine books and accounts. Unregistered unions would be liable for unlimited damages, as would employers' associations. Registered unions, however, would be limited in the amount of compensation for which they were liable. This would be related to their membership; for example, for less than 5,000 members, £5,000; 5,000 – 25,000, £25,000; 25,000 – 100,000, £50,000; 100,000 or more, £100,000.

The second pillar of the Act is '*the right to join or not to join*' a trade union. While this represents a considerable step forward in a legal sense, the unions have managed to organise and flourish without it for many years. There is however, the anomaly that in socialist Britain in 1951 it was legal for an employer to refuse to recognise or allow a trades union on his premises, while in the capitalist United States in the same period, this was an illegal employer practice. A Labour Government would have given the legal right *to join* a trades union; the Conservatives conceded this right, but added the right 'not to join'. This has been called a false antithesis, and a 'charter for blacklegs and non-unionists'. It is argued that the right to join trade unions helps to strengthen collective bargaining by strengthening unions. This was the argument of the Donovan Commission, which pointed out that the right to join was a social right as it strengthened the organisation, whereas the right not to join was an individual right and could be socially divisive.

Trade unionists resent working and paying for a trade union which nego-
tiates better wages and working conditions, while non-unionists, or 'free-
riders', enjoy the benefits without any of the sacrifices or effort. For many
years it has been common for unionists to refuse to work alongside non-
unionists, and they have at times struck on the principle of '100 per cent'
membership. This might now become an 'illegal action'. The Conservative
reply to this is that they believe in trade unionism, but defend the right of
the individual not to join or be coerced into joining. In this view, they were
probably influenced by films such as 'The Angry Silence' where a worker is
sent to Coventry by his workmates, and by newspaper accounts of the operations of closed shops. The argument here is that if a man refuses to be a union
member in a closed shop industry or occupation, he is denied entry to the
job or industry.

The Act forbids the pre-entry closed shop, where only union or approved
members can enter, and the post-entry closed shop, where all relevant workers
must be union members, becomes difficult to maintain. Provision is made in
the Act for an agency shop: employers or unions may apply to the NIRC,
for reference to the CIR, which in turn holds a ballot to see if the workers
concerned want an agency shop to which workers must belong, unless they
have conscientious objections and pay contributions to agreed charities.
Agency shops can also be formed on a voluntary basis. There is also an
approved closed shop for unions such as the Seamen's, and Equity for actors,
which argue that the special circumstances of their work and membership
make it necessary for them to have a closed shop.

We can compare these provisions with those of the USA. The National
Labor Relations Act gives 'the right to self-organisation' under Section 7
and the right to engage in... concerted activities for the purpose of collective
bargaining or other mutual aid or protection, and the right to refrain from
any or all of such activities' except where there is an agreement requiring
membership under a union-security agreement. This agreement is of the
'post-entry' closed shop type and workers are normally given thirty days
grace before being required to join.

The third main pillar is the *enforceability of collective agreements*. As we
have noted previously, most collective agreements in British industrial relations were not drawn up by the parties to the agreement with legal enforcement in mind (Ford Motor Co. *v.* AUEW, 1969). Under the Act, agreements
which have been made in writing, and which do not contain a clause stating
that the agreement is not legally enforceable 'shall be conclusively presumed
to be intended by the parties to it to be a legally enforceable contract'
(Section 34). Where such agreements are legally enforceable, it shall be an
'unfair industrial practice' to breach the agreement.

The Conservative Government argued that unions should be under the same law as other citizens who had to honour contracts when they signed them. A union would then have to 'use its best endeavours' to prevent any strike in breach of the agreement. This would usually apply to unofficial strikes, but might affect official strikes if the employer thought that the agreement had been broken. There is also the question as to action for damages against the party which 'induced' a breach of contract. The unions argue that collective agreements are not like normal commercial contracts, but involve human relationships and continual adjustment and negotiation.

Experts in industrial relations have said that the unions who reach agreement with employers seldom break them; therefore legal enforceability is not needed. Again, the local factory groups who come out on unofficial strike will not be bound, or influenced, by such agreements. The solution in this case is not the enforceable agreement which would be legally unenforceable, but the reform of collective bargaining and the provisions for speedy local conciliation and arbitration.

The Government view was that the union itself should be the responsible party, and that the Act would strengthen 'responsible trade unionism' by persuading unions to exercise greater control over the actions of their members. Presumably, a union might have to threaten, and perhaps expel or fine, members who were in breach of union rules or of the collective contract. Unions such as the Steelworkers have disciplined members in recent years (in 1959 several lay officials were removed from office for leading an unofficial strike), but few unions have done this, and it becomes virtually impossible when and if several thousand workers all claim responsibility for the breach and deny that they were led by others. It has been argued that a 'go-slow' would be a breach of contract, but this would be difficult to prove in practice.

The Act sets out to follow US practice. Section 8(d) of the NLR Act requires that the parties meet, 'confer in good faith' and put the agreement in writing. Both parties are obliged to bargain collectively, although they are not required to agree. Strict procedures are laid down regarding observance of the contract, and notice must be given of termination. This means that most strikes in the USA are official, and that they take place at the end of the contract, before the new one is agreed. However, the existence of strict contracts seems not to prevent a certain number of unofficial or 'wildcat' strikes from taking place. Such breaches are seldom brought to court.

A fourth main pillar refers to *sympathetic strike action*. Strikes or threats of strikes may become 'unfair industrial practices' if they are intended to support an industrial dispute which is not the direct concern of the union. This is known as the secondary boycott or strike. Factory X may be on strike and the workers of Factory Y decide to stop sending materials or contracted supplies there, or threaten to do so. The case would have to be argued that the Factory Y workers were doing so to assist factory X workers in putting pressure on their employers. The legal point is that the Y workers are not a party to the dispute.

There are a whole range of unfair industrial practices, such as strikes undertaken to persuade the employer that a worker or workers should be union members, or to force union recognition, or to have a worker dismissed, or to enforce a closed shop or agency shop, or to persuade other workers to stop delivering goods to a firm on strike (the case of the secondary boycott described above). Sanctions for unfair industrial practices could include the payment of compensation to the employer for losses incurred.

The NLR Act in the USA has a number of clauses relating to 'unfair labor practices'. But the employer is forbidden, under the 1959 Act, from entering into a 'hot cargo' agreement with the employees. Such an agreement stipulates that the employer will not do business with an employer that the union has labelled as 'unfair'. This practice has usually been found in trucking and construction.

Peaceful picketing is allowed as before under the Act. This is defined as 'peacefully communicating' or informing workers that the premises are strike-bound. The US Act goes much further in defining the activities of pickets, and labels as restraint or coercion acts such as mass picketing to prevent entry of non-strikers, acts of force or violence or threats against non-strikers, threats against non-strikers' jobs and other related threats.

A fifth pillar introduces *'cooling-off' periods* and *compulsory strike ballots.* There had been much public concern over 'lightning' or unofficial strikes, which appeared to many Conservative MPs and newspapers as precipitate and damaging to the firm and the economy. They were convinced that if some delaying pause could be introduced between the initial demand for a strike and the strike itself, this would give time for consideration, assessment, a possible change of mind, or a solution to the dispute. The Donovan Commission had considered a 'cooling-off' period, which could be introduced for the Government by the then Minister of Labour, through an application for an injunction. The injunction would ask for work to continue, and the strike or lockout to be postponed, for a period of some sixty days. This would allow the negotiations to continue; if they were unsuccessful, the strike or dispute could be resumed after the end of the 'cooling-off' period.

Donovan points out that injunctions were granted in the USA in 24 cases. In all but one the stand-still period was imposed. In sixteen cases a settlement was reached; in seven there were stoppages during and after. During the standstill the USFM & CS tries to reach an agreed solution, and can ballot the union membership. In none of the above cases did the employees vote to accept the employer's latest offer. Donovan was against a 'cooling-off' period for British industrial relations. The British strike figure was much lower than the American, and the DEP had wide powers to intervene in strikes and disputes, to conciliate and arbitrate. A 'cooling-off' period might impose rigidity on this flexible system.

The Labour Government had not been impressed by the Donovan argument on this issue in 1969. 'In Place of Strife' said that unofficial strikes were such a problem that time should be given for consultation and negotiation. They proposed a 'conciliation pause', to be introduced by the Secretary of State for Labour when the effect of the strike would be serious. The DEP would take action; if unsuccessful, the Secretary of State would issue an order, after due warning, to both sides. They would be required to resume work and postpone industrial action for 28 days. Trade union objections led to the Labour government dropping the plan, but proof of its durability is the eagerness with which it was resurrected by the 1970 Conservative Government.

The 1971 Act also proposed a compulsory ballot as part of the emergency procedures. The application for a 'cooling-off' period might be accompanied by an application to NIRC, if the Secretary of State had reasons for thinking that the workers in the strike threatened firm or industry were more reluctant to strike than their leaders, would welcome the employer's last offer, or would be badly affected by the strike. The Secretary of State would make the application after he had consulted all available opinion, and ascertained that the dispute would affect the national economy or security. In the event of the application being granted, industrial action would have to stop while the ballot was being taken.

Donovan had rejected the idea of a compulsory ballot. The suggestion that a secret ballot would show that workers were less militant than their leaders was said to be invalidated by experience of such ballots in Canada and the USA. The great majority of compulsory ballots supported the union leadership. The Commission's other objection was that the ballot, if affirmative, could prolong the strike and hamper negotiations. 'In Place of Strife' gave the Secretary of State discretionary powers to demand a ballot where major strike action was threatened, and where he had doubts about the support of union members for the action. The Labour Government had abandoned this proposal by mid 1969.

The sixth pillar provides for the *selective statutory enforcement of procedure agreements* in certain areas. Cases may arise where a company has different premises and unions to deal with in different areas. The varying industrial relations agreements may be causing irritation and unrest. The Secretary of State may apply to NIRC for an agreement to cover all the employees, on the grounds that the existing agreements were procedurally defective, absent or unsuitable. The application would only be made after the Secreatry had had full consultations with the parties concerned.

The unions objected to the enforcement of procedure agreements, as they objected to agreements being made legally enforceable without the consent of the parties. They feared that the imposition of a procedure agreement would be followed by legal pressure to negotiate on wages and conditions, which they claimed would be mainly in the interests of the employer.

The Donovan Commission pointed out that there already existed *ad hoc* legislation, under Section 8 of the Terms and Conditions of Employment Act, by which the Industrial Court could enforce upon employers recognised terms and conditions. The Commission noted that a number of countries did have collective agreements enforceable at law, but as this procedure was invariably more used by the employer than by the union, certain standards for the employee were guaranteed by law. Employers had to observe these standards whether they were signatories to the agreement, or members of an association. In general, the Commission was opposed to the statutory enforcement of procedure agreements for the same reasons as it had opposed the legal enforcement of the collective contract.

The seventh pillar borrows directly from the USA the concept of the *statutory bargaining agent and unit*. The intention is that the approved collective bargaining procedures described above should be negotiated by an organisation which represents a particular firm or group of workers specified in the agreement. Historically, the parties have come to an agreement between themselves. Inter-union disputes over which union should represent which groups or occupations of workers have been dealt with through the Bridlington Agreement (1939) of the TUC. This marked out the spheres of influence of different unions, and set up a TUC committee to deal with inter-union disputes, whether over membership, 'poaching' or strike-breaking. Section 44 of the Act, which deals with the recognition of the sole bargaining agent, allows the voluntary system to continue. In the event of an unresolved dispute, an 'application may be made to the Industrial Court for reference to the Commission'. The Court would receive applications from one or more trade unions, or one or more employers, or from both jointly, or from the Secretary of State. The application should only be made after full consultation with all parties concerned. The questions examined by the Court would relate to the definition of the bargaining unit, which groups of workers were included and why, and the definition of the bargaining agent, the union or committee which would represent and bargain for the specific groups of workers. The Court would satisfy itself that the parties had tried to settle the matter themselves before the CIR was asked to investigate, possibly by defining the bargaining unit and making a report to the Court and the interested parties. After that a ballot of the workers concerned could be held, so that their consent or views could be established. The Commission would have to be satisfied that the workers formed a common interest group, either through work, training, experience of qualifications, that they 'would have the support of a substantial proportion of the employees comprised in the bargaining unit' (Sec. 48, (4)(5)).

This section was attacked by the unions as a 'charter for breakaway unions' and an open encouragement to the splinter groups in some unions. They argued that the NIRC had discretion on whether to refer recognition or bargaining issues to the CIR or not; that the NIRC would inquire whether the bargaining agents were competent, but would not ask about the firm's labour management. They objected to the new statutory powers given to the CIR and preferred it in its older, voluntary role.

This section of the Act, including the terms 'bargaining unit' and 'bargaining agent', is borrowed from the NLR Act of the USA. The NLRB did much work in the late 1930s in specifying these terms and supervising elections in plants. Section 9(b) says that the NLRB shall decide 'the unit appropriate' whether 'employer unit, craft unit, plant unit, or subdivision thereof', professional or non-professional. This function of the NLRB has done much to mould the bargaining structure in industrial relations, so that the most widely found representation is 'one plant, one union'. Secret ballots can also be held, on a petition signed by 30 per cent or more of the employees, to withdraw the certification of the bargaining representative, and therefore his authority to act for them.

The NLRB holds its bargaining unit/agent elections under strict conditions. Employers are not allowed to threaten employees, either with loss of jobs or closure, or by questioning them, or by making wage increases 'deliberately timed to discourage employees from forming or joining a union' (Sec. 8(a)(1)). There is a lengthy catalogue of unfair labour practices of employers.

The eighth pillar concerns *rights of unions to recognition*. The whole of the Industrial Relations Act rests on the assumption, an important assumption, that trade unions would register under the Act. If they remained unregistered the privileges of the Act would be denied them, as would the immunities under the law; they would not be able to apply for the approved closed shop or the agency shop; would be liable for unlimited compensation, whereas registered unions would have limits; would not be able to apply for recognition as a sole bargaining agent; and their rights in using the strike weapon would be severely restricted, as it would be an 'unfair industrial practice' for those individuals or organisations to induce or threaten breach of contract, to threaten or call a strike, or to have a worker dismissed or make him join a union.

The most important aspect of the above section is that the 1971 Act repealed and replaced the Acts of 1906 and 1967. The immunities previously conferred under those Acts were revived and extended, but they only applied to those organisations, of unions and employers, who had registered. Unregistered bodies suffered financial loss through loss of tax protection on pension funds. They were also liable for a whole range of unfair industrial practices, as well as for the legal remedies against these practices. Employers or individual workers could bring actions against unions, organisations or individuals. Fines could be levied against the offenders. The Government has argued that the legal enforcement of fines and compensation is a civil, not a criminal matter, but the distinction has little meaning in law if the Court decides to enforce the fine or payment. Refusal to appear before the Court can be treated as contempt of court and the offender can be fined or imprisoned.

To some extent the enforcement of the Act resembles the NLR Act, which is administered by the NLRB. The Board has the power to call and examine witnesses, issue subpoenas and exercise the full powers of a court of law generally, including punishment for perjury while giving testimony. Section 12 states that 'any person who shall wilfully resist, prevent, impede, or interfere with any member of the Board or its agencies in the performance of duties pursuant to this Act shall be punished by a fine of not more than $5000 or by imprisonment for not more than one year, or both'. The affinity here with the British Industrial Relations Act is marked; the Board insists that, except for the foregoing Section, the NLR Act 'is not a criminal statute. Its purpose is entirely remedial'. This was the tone of Mr Robert Carr when he introduced his Bill in the House of Commons.

7 Strikes and the Act

The Conservative Government of 1970 expected great changes in industrial relations to result from the passing of the Industrial Relations Act. Strikes would decrease, the number of man-days lost would decrease, and militant shop steward groups would lose their power to force through inflationary wage increases at plant level.

As events turned out, this was too simplistic a view. The Act raised the question of social control through the force of law. Yet the law was being imposed on large groups of workers, against the wishes of their elected leaders in the unions (though admittedly on the mandate of a Parliamentary majority, however small). The new law came at a time when many workers were more conscious of, and troubled by, inflation, than at any time in the past. This was a spur to their wage demands. There were also far reaching technological changes and shifts in market demand. The latter led to a rundown in the number of miners and to many pit closures; the former led to containerisation in the docks and to the development of natural gas. Both resulted in the contraction of the railways. These circumstances combined to lead to large scale industrial trouble in 1972.

The climate of industrial relations had also been worsened by the 'abrasive' policies pursued by the 1970 Government in its first two years. The Conservatives had made a political virtue of their opposition to incomes policy, which they thought both unworkable and destructive of union leadership. Unemployment rose to a million and tax changes favoured the richer citizens. They also set out to pursue a negative incomes policy by attempting, as Mr. Barber said in January 1971, 'a substantial and progressive de-escalation in the rate of pay settlements'. This led to the pay policy of N-1, with N being the percentage increase which the previous pay settlement group had reached. The Government, as public paymaster, was to set an example by saying 'no' to inflationary claims in the public sector. This policy led to a series of official confrontations between Government and unions, a great rise in the number of days lost through strikes, and the discovery, by the Government and the courts, of how difficult it is to enforce law in industrial relations.

The Miners' Strike

By mid September the National Union of Mineworkers (NUM) was asking for minimum pay of £35 for face workers, £28 for others underground and

£26 for surface workers. The National Coal Board (NCB) offered 7 per cent, far below the union demands, and the union refused to negotiate. The NUM started to put pressure on the NCB by holding a special conference which recommended that the union should withdraw from all joint committees, ban overtime and hold a strike ballot. The last decision was the most important, as the NUM had recently changed its rules to allow strike action to be taken if 55 per cent were in favour instead of the two-thirds previously needed. The ballot showed 59 per cent in favour of striking.

The NUM anticipated the result by planning to alter union rules to protect funds, in the event of being liable for damages under the Industrial Relations Act. After the ballot in favour, a national strike was called for on 9 January.

The national press did not seem alarmed at the prospect. Commentators wrote that there were coal stocks sufficient for a number of weeks, and a settlement would be reached before then. Few thought that the miners would stay out for weeks, or that the strike and picketing tactics would develop as they did. Events showed that they had underestimated the tenacity and solidarity of the miners. It had been thought that the electricity workers had settled quickly in December because of the pressure of public opinion directed against them, and that the miners would do the same. But community pressures worked for the miners, as most of them lived in tightly knit communities which supported them in the strike, while the public sympathised with the demand of the miners for more pay, which they had not done with the electricity workers.

By early January the NCB had increased its pay offer from 7 per cent to 7.9 per cent. Attempts by the Department of Employment to conciliate proved abortive. The strike began with the miners picketing the mines, as they were allowed to do under the law of picketing. They then widened their operations to picketing NCB regional headquarters and offices, and there were complaints – of abuse and of being kicked – from female clerks (not members of the NUM, and not in dispute with the NCB) who went to work in the offices. Police were called in to prevent further trouble.

Picketing

Picketing and the turbulent scenes on the picket lines were shown night after night on television. The close-ups of girls weeping, or being interviewed for their reactions to the miners' picketing methods, led to questions in the House of Commons. Significantly, back bench MPs reserved most of their indignation until the strike was over. Questions in March 1972 about the abuse of law by pickets brought the answer that most picketing was peaceful, though some incidents had given cause for concern. The law would be reviewed. Conservative MPs came under vigorous questioning in their constituencies and they in turn pressed the Government. The official reply given by Cabinet Ministers, particularly Sir Geoffrey Howe, Solicitor-General, was that the right to picket was not a right to threaten, intimidate, assault or obstruct. Anyone doing any of these things while picketing was breaking the law and would be dealt with by the police.

In fact, though the police were heavily engaged in trying to control pickets and protect other workers, they were unsuccessful against large numbers of determined pickets, and numbers of police were injured in scuffles. No miners were imprisoned, and the numbers fined are unknown, though they were few in number.

Later strike tactics were to move the pickets away from the mines, where they had earlier succeeded in preventing the mining deputies from going underground (the deputies were in a separate union, NACODS, which was not in dispute with the NCB) and in refusing to send miners underground to service essential machinery, which they had agreed to do during a strike. The NUM did issue statements asking for safety work to be done in pits, but this instruction was widely ignored at local level. The NCB feared that millions of pounds 'worth of machinery would be ruined and many pits would have to be permanently closed.

Apart from the impact on the public through television, the strike did not have much effect on industry in the first phase, although the Government did appeal for economy in the use of coal. The strike began to bite when the NUM pickets appeared outside open cast coal sites, coal depots, ports and power stations. It is academic to argue whether the picketing was illegal or not, as the Government took no visible action and the police spent most of their time trying to protect and regulate traffic passing to and from these places. Lawyers, though, might have had some difficulty in proving an offence if the matter had been brought to court.

The tactics of the miners were to stop coal from being used as much as possible. The layman might have said, 'The miners dug the coal. They were paid for this. The coal had been sold by the NCB to dealers, and was in coal depots, or in transit to ports or power stations. Therefore the miners were engaged in illegal picketing.' Yet this tactic had been used in the dustmen's strike of 1970, when the strikers picketed refuse dumps, and tried to stop householders from dumping their own rubbish and shopkeepers from hiring lorries to remove their refuse.

By the 21 January, the Secretary of State for Employment was trying to use his traditional role and persuade the two sides to negotiate. He was unsuccessful. He tried again on 9 February and the NCB raised its pay offer considerably. This was rejected by the NUM, who had now begun to see signs that the strike was taking effect.

The final, and most effective strike strategy, was the picketing of the power stations. The miners did not work there, nor was the Electricity Board in dispute with the miners or their own electricity supply workers. The miners claimed that the power stations used coal and they wanted to stop any supplies of coal from going in. But the ultimate objective was to close down the power stations through denying them supplies of water and oil. This was done by stopping all lorries entering, and asking the drivers to turn back. 'Asking' is a euphemism for some of the tactics used, but the Government insisted that if picketing was not 'peaceful' then the police on the spot could enforce the law. Other unions were persuaded to help the miners in their strike; most lorry drivers were members of the T & GWU and they agreed not to go through the picket lines and deliver any supplies. Railwaymen refused to deliver wagons of coal, but as the power stations had large stocks of coal this would not have been crucial to electricity supply. The important point was the stopping of oil and water deliveries. The miners were also helped by the Engineers, who staged a one-day strike and put some 12,000 demonstrators round one large power station. The police abandoned their attempts to keep the gates open for lorries and advised the power station managers to close the gates for the day.

Strikers and Social Secutiry

The NUM announced at the beginning of the strike that they did not have enough money for strike pay. (This position can be contrasted with that of the T & GWU and the AUEW, who paid out £5–£6 weekly for strikers). However, the miners were facing the prospects of a lengthy national strike and they had never visualised supporting large numbers of members and their families for any period. Miners' families were advised to apply for social security, described by one cynic as 'the national strike fund'. Strikers cannot claim state monies unless they are in urgent need of help; some were and received some funds. The families of strikers could and did apply. No detailed figures were available showing the number of miners who were single, what proportion were married, and how many had children of school age eligible for social security. Legally, a miner's family with two children between 11 and 15 years could receive £15–£16. We do not know what numbers could draw the maximum social security, but we do know that the weekly amount drawn by miners' dependents from social security was about £1,000,000 weekly. Some £5½ million was paid out in the six weeks of the strike, much more than any union could have paid from a strike fund (for example, the T & GWV, with nearly 1½ million members, paid out £501,720 in 1969).

This money was paid by the State for the use of strikers' families. Until 1971, families receiving social security could also have other sources of income up to £4 weekly. This was known as 'disregarded income'. The practical effects of this for trade unions were that if they paid out strike pay of £4, and their members had no other monies coming in, they would receive the £4 strike pay in addition to social security payments received by the family. This was changed in March 1971 by the Conservative Government, who reduced the 'disregarded income' from £4 to £1. In such a situation, as a miner's leader pointed out, to pay strike pay is simply to transfer money from the union funds to the State insurance funds.

Another issue posed by social security payments related to an NUM request to the Social Security Commission. They asked the Commission if they could pay 'subsistence money' to members on picket duty. The Commission decided that they could and, using the Civil Service formula for meal allowances, said that the union could pay pickets £1.25 daily. This decision meant that the young, single pickets, as well as others, could receive money which was under 'expenses' not 'income'. This helped the effectiveness of the union's picketing, as the younger and more active members had an extra inducement to do picket duty, and five days' picketing would bring as much as a single man would receive in unemployment money.

Large numbers of men also went 'sick' before the strike began. This entitled them to draw sickness benefit for the period they were absent. The Department of Social Security has a regulation which states that officials should investigate cases of men on strike reporting sick, and possibly getting the opinion of a second doctor, but in cases of large numbers reporting this becomes virtually impossible to check.

The Industrial Relations Act and the Miners' Strike

The Industrial Relations Act, on which such high hopes had been pinned, did nothing to prevent the strike or change its course. Some critics argued that it had the contrary effect of lengthening the strike and raising the total award paid to the miners.

The strike followed the procedures laid down in the Act although some of these did not become law until 28 February, after the strike ended. It was an official strike called by the Executive, which was endorsed by a ballot of members producing a majority of 59 per cent for the strike. The issue which caused most argument, in Parliament and elsewhere, was the manner in which the picketing was carried out. Picketing is the right to stand outside the premises in which one works, for the purpose of informing people about the strike. As Sir Geoffrey Howe stated, it is not a right to threaten, intimidate, assault or obstruct. There were a number of complaints made to the newspapers, radio and television that threats, assault and obstruction had taken place. Cabinet Ministers said that the picketing was mainly 'peaceful'. If there were breaches of the law, the police on the spot could take action. Police action did prevent some fighting taking place, though there were counter complaints from the miners of excessive force by the police.

Accounts from different areas about the picketing show the difficulty of enforcing the law against large numbers. Private cars trying to enter premises found their way blocked, and were pushed back by crowds, even while they were in first gear. Cars were rocked and banged and the occupants intimidated. The police were unable to press any charges, though some cases went to court. In one case where the miners were found not guilty by a jury, there were 450 police facing some 3,000 pickets. Evidence was given by the police that they were referred to by some miners as 'the enemy' and that boots would be used on them. Miners were wearing their pit boots with steel toe-caps. The difficulty from the Court's point of view in hearing such a case, was that, if a policeman were pushed over and kicked unconscious, he would not be able to give a positive identification of his assailant. There was also the practical difficulty that, if a miner or miners had been imprisoned for violence while picketing, this might have prolonged the strike.

It could be said, when comparing the Post Office strike, which was unsuccessful, with the miners' strike, which was a spectacular success, that both strikes had public sympathy, but the miners had public sympathy and industrial muscle. As the strike turned on the stranglehold which the miners were able to exercise over the nation's power supplies through the effectiveness of their picketing, the muscle had some power.

The Wage Settlement

We have already described the two pay offers, the second of 7.9 per cent, which the NUM had received by early January. These were refused and the strike began. At this point, with the advantage of hindsight, we can point out some of the mistakes which the NCB negotiators seemed to make. Firstly, after the strike started, the NCB withdrew its latest offer, an action which seemed to stiffen the miners' resolve to continue. Secondly, though this was the fault of the Government rather than the Coal Board, the NCB was negotiating with the miners on the basis of the then financial position of the industry, which was many millions of pounds in deficit. It might have been better had the NCB reached agreement with the miners on a figure of around 12 per cent, some $4\frac{1}{2}$ per cent above the Government 'norm' for pay increases, and then asked the Government for financial help. As events developed and the industry faced a large scale shutdown, the Government became increasingly concerned about reaching a settlement. Efforts at conciliation failed, and a state of emergency was declared, giving the Government wide powers to ration electricity through power cuts and other measures. This caused great disruption in industry, as the Regional Boards switched off power by areas in rotation. Domestic consumers were often left in the dark and candle manufacturers made large profits. These events increased the pressure on Parliament to settle the dispute, as industry went on short-time working, with over 1 million workers laid off.

The Government set up a court of inquiry under Lord Wilberforce, which pointed out that the miners had asked for increases of £8, £9, and £5 respectively for surface, underground and power loader workers. The Board had offered £1.80 for surface and £1.75 for other grades. Improved offers were rejected, including £3, £3.50 and £2.75 for the above grades. The miners reduced their demands to £6, £7 and £4. No agreement was reached

Wilberforce argued that the miners' work was unique in its roughness, physical exertion and danger. The miners had co-operated in the run-down of their industry for 15 years, with pits closing and the number of miners reduced from 700,000 to 290,000, and collieries from 800 to 300. Productivity had increased greatly, by 75 per cent in the fifteen year period. The increase in productivity had been partly due to mechanisation, and the Power Loading Agreement which changed the method of payment from the piece-rates which caused friction and strikes, to the day wage system based on power loading. This reduced wage drift and unofficial strikes.

The discontent of the miners was partly due to the relative fall in earnings, from near the top of the manual worker table to near the middle. With the greater emphasis on relative earnings in the middle and late 1960s this had been a festering sore to the miners.

The conclusion was that miners' earnings were too low when compared to their contribution to productivity under difficult conditions. They were 'a special case' and should receive a substantial rise. As the NCB had begun the previous year with a deficit of £35 million, and the NUM revised claim would amount to £100 million a year, the Government might give financial assistance by tackling the high interest and depreciation charges in the coal industry, together about £90 million. Price increases might be counterproductive.

Wilberforce thought that the NCB offer was 'perfectly fair', based on their statutory and financial position. The miners' case was 'logical'. The money to fill the gap between the two positions would be found from 'the public, through the Government'. Surface workers were offered £5, underground £6, face workers on power loading agreement £4.50. This award came close to the NUM revised position of £6, £7 and £4.

By this time, however, the miners had the Government and industry 'over a barrel' and did not accept the Wilberforce Report as it stood. The Prime Minister, Mr Heath, continued the negotiations at Downing Street, and the miners were given extra concessions costing the coal industry another £8 million. The strike had lasted seven weeks, from early January until late February. It was hailed as an outstanding victory by the miners, belated retribution for their defeat in 1926, a breach in the Government's wages dam, and a green light to the militants in the unions.

One important result of the strike was that the NCB ran into a serious financial deficit. The Government then agreed to write off a number of the statutory debts of the Board, and the industry received financial support amounting to some £500 million. This was another departure from the Conservative philosophy of 1970, and showed how the miners' strike power had been directed against the Government, who alone could meet their wage claim, and not against the NCB, which did not have the money. The decision to finance miners' pay from national taxation was inevitable, but it showed the way for other unions in the public sector, such as the railwaymen and the dockers, who had the power to mount and win national strikes. The Government were aware that the wages dam had been breached, though they kept insisting that the miners' award was due to their being 'a very special case'. Most unions felt that their claims were in a special category, as later events showed.

The Rail Strike

Soon after the miners had begun their national strike, the railwaymen had their pay claim rejected. The British Railways Board argued that the pay agreement should run until its expiry date in May 1972, The Associated Society of Locomotive Engineers and Firemen (ASLEF), the most highly paid of the three rail unions, narrowly defeated a strike call on their national executive by two votes. Negotiations continued in March when the Railways Board made an offer of 11 per cent. We should note here that this was much higher than the original 7 per cent offered the miners, demonstrating the national effect that the miners' success had on the level of wage settlements.

Like the miners, the railwaymen felt that they were part of a declining industry. The railways, like the mines, had been nationalised in 1947, without any dramatic improvement in industrial relations. From the mid 1950s the railways had ceased to pay their way, and the rail unions faced an increasing stream of redundancies. By the early 1960s there were complaints of 100.000 redundancies. The Beeching Plan had further reduced the number of railway lines, trains and stations.

A further point of comparison between railways and mines is that neither were really on strike against their Boards. Neither board had sufficient money to pay substantial wage increases, and a rise in the price of coal or rail travel would simply reduce the revenue, due to substitution of other fuels or methods of travel. The rail unions had earlier established the principle that wage increases should be paid, even if the Railways Board had a deficit. It was agreed that if the State willed the end (to give the railmen a decent wage) then it must will the means (give the railways a subsidy or financial help in meeting or writing off depreciation and interest charges).

By 11 April the railways said that they could not increase their offer and the railway unions announced a work-to-rule six days later. This was held up while the Government appointed an independent arbitrator. His offer was $1\frac{1}{2}$ per cent above that of the railways and was rejected by the unions. The work-to-rule began on 20 April and the intention of the unions was to disrupt train services by interpreting the rules of work so strictly that trains would be delayed and the travelling public driven as close as possible to angry protests. The railmen would achieve disruption while receiving their basic pay, which is one reason why the work-to-rule is known as 'the strike on the job'. The pay claim was complicated by inter-union arguments over differentials. While all three rail unions wanted a £20 minimum basic wage, the engine drivers wanted their traditional differential over other grades to be observed. The whole pay claim amounted to a 14 per cent increase.

Negotiations followed their now familiar course. Newspapers published photographs of crowded stations, and television interviewed irate travellers. Trade union officials told the interviewer nightly, 'It is not our wish to in-convenience the travelling public. We hope that reason will prevail'. Trans-lated into lay language, this meant that there would be no strike if the men's demands were met. The greater the discomfort or delay suffered by rail travellers, the greater the pressure on Parliament to settle the dispute by various means. When the traditional methods of negotiation, conciliation and arbitration had failed, the Government used the new weapon in its armoury, the Industrial Relations Act, and went to the NIRC to ask for a three week 'cooling-off' period. This move was a departure from the pattern of rail pay settlements in the past, where lengthy negotiations and strike threats usually led to conciliation attempts and final settlements in 10 Downing Street. The Conservative Government went to the NIRC under pressure from MPs who wanted to justify the passing of the Industrial Rela-tions Act. The application for a cooling-off period of twenty-one days was made by Mr Macmillan, Secretary of State for Employment, under Section 138 (Emergency Proceedings) of the Act, which states that, in contemplation or furtherance of an industrial action, consisting of a strike, any irregular industrial action short of a strike, or a lock-out, has begun or is likely to begin'. The Act states that, if the Court grants a cooling-off order, no strikes or strike organisation or threats of strikes can be made for that period of time. The Secretary of State, in his application, has to show that the industrial action would either endanger lives or public health, or 'be gravely injurious to the national economy, ... imperil national security, or create a serious risk of public disorder'.

The Government's case was that the work-to-rule – strict rule observance and a ban on overtime and rest day working – constituted irregular industrial action; that the industrial action should be temporarily stopped or the national economy would be seriously affected. The three rail unions, ASLEF, the NUR and TSSA, were named as respondents. Mr. Macmillan asked for a cooling-off period of twenty-one days during which normal working should be resumed. The course of negotiations from February to April were described. Neither side had referred the dispute to the arbitration machinery contained in an agreement of May 1956. Attempts at mediation by a third party resulted in an improved offer of $12\frac{1}{2}$ per cent instead of 11 per cent. The unions had rejected this, as they had rejected appeals by the Secretary of State to suspend industrial action and ballot the membership.

This was the first cooling-off application to appear before the NIRC, which agreed that irregular industrial action had taken place, that this should be temporarily discontinued so that settlement attempts could be made, and that the economy would be seriously affected. The NIRC decided that fourteen days, not twenty-one, would be sufficient for cooling-off. This decision underlined the statement by the NIRC that the Court was not a 'rubberstamp' for the Government.

The Government application to the NIRC was attacked by the Opposition after Mr Macmillan had made a statement in Parliament. Mr Prentice (Labour) thought the application would stop a continuing dialogue, asked what steps would be taken to settle the dispute, and whether cooling-off could be ordered where men were working to their normal contract and no strike had taken place. The Speaker intervened, warning that the matter was before a court, and was therefore *sub judice*. Mr Prentice asked a number of questions about the dispute, including the definition of normal and abnormal working of the rule book. After a number of questions had brought words without answers, Mr Steel (Liberal) asked the Secretary of State 'What is he asking the court for?' Mr Macmillan: 'I am advised that while the court is sitting I should not go into detail'. Mr Callaghan (Labour) objected that 'important semi-political issues' were being removed from the control of the House. The Government should not be able to make 'secret applications'. (House of Commons, 19 April 1972).

The cooling-off period failed to achieve any settlement, although the NUR offered to split the difference between the Railways Board offer and the union claim. The Board replied by offering the £20 minimum rate originally claimed by the unions, but from 5 June instead of 1 May. This would have reduced the overall cost of the claim to the railways. Matters were further complicated by London Transport's offer to their unions to pay from 1 May whatever basic rate increases were agreed by the Railways Board. This subsidiary offer weakened the negotiating stand of British Rail, which was aware of the Government's intention to try and hold wage increases down to a level of 8 per cent, and which, like the NCB had a massive financial deficit that would grow worse with a large wage increase, while a large price increase might be counter-productive and might not be officially approved. The Board was in a bargaining straitjacket. The unions were aware of this, but like the miners, they were negotiating with the Government, not their employers.

The failure of the cooling-off period forced the Government to use the IR Act for a second time. They made an application to the NIRC under Section 141 (1)(a)(c) of the Act, which states:

(a)   that in contemplation or furtherance of an industrial dispute a strike or any irregular industrial action short of a strike has begun or is likely to begin ...

(c)   that there are reasons for doubting whether the workers who are taking part or are expected to take part in the strike or other industrial action are or would be taking part in it in accordance with their wishes, and whether they have had an adequate opportunity of indicating their wishes in this respect.

The application for an emergency order was made on 11 May 1972 on the grounds that railway workers had not been properly consulted on the pay offer made by the Railways Board. The course of the pay negotiations were described, the union decision to ban overtime, rest day and Sunday working, and work to rule. Improved pay offers had been made through mediation and by the Railways Board, the latest refusal being on 11 May. Grave injury was being caused to the economy and to London commuters by the dispute. The application set out the proposed question for the ballot, and examples of the proposed pay increases.

The NIRC said that the unions' instruction to work to rule was a breach of contract, with the intention of making the trains run late, and seriously affecting the commercial viability of the railways, although the Board had conceded that refusal to work Sundays or rest days was not a breach of contract. The Secretary of State had said there were reasons for doubting whether the workers taking part in industrial action had been fully consulted. He had made an error in suggesting that the TSSA had ordered a work-to-rule, as it had told its members to observe the terms of their contract, but this did not invalidate the application. Surprisingly, the Court ruled that the Secretary of State did not need to give the reasons for doubting that union members had been consulted.

This last point led to arguments in newspapers and the mass media. Critics said that the Secretary of State had not properly consulted the unions on this matter. They would have told him how they knew, through union meetings, that their members supported the decision of their executives. It was argued that the effects of the strike on the economy called for a political judgement and a political decision. Finally, it was pointed out that in the USA, from which the legislation had been borrowed, the emergency procedure ballots invariably produced a large majority supporting the union, on the grounds that the men had nothing to lose, and something to gain, by backing up their unions' demands. The ballot showed overwhelming support for the question authorised by the NIRC:

> In the light of the BRB pay offer (about which you are being informed by the BRB), do you wish to take part in further industrial action? Yes, No?

The railwaymen voted 'yes' by over 5 to 1, and this was the second failure of the Act to settle the dispute. This proved, as *The Times* said, that 'in an industrial conflict men back their unions... there must be no hesitation in negotiating a railways settlement' (*The Times*, 1 June 1972).

The Dock Strike

After the failure of the Industrial Relations Act to deal with the rail strike, the Government were in a worse position with the dockers. The dockers had always been one of the most militant groups in the labour force, tightly knit and with long traditions of working class solidarity. Neither their union (the T&GWU) nor the law had much influence on the docks. During the period of incomes policy from 1965–70, dockers' earnings had risen by over 70 per cent against the average in manufacturing industry of some 40 per cent. This was due to the ability of the dockers to threaten and to mount short unofficial strikes under their unofficial leaders.

The main issue in the docks dispute appeared as a resentment of the loss of jobs caused by containerisation, which, by enabling goods to be stored in large containers in either factory or storage plant, allowed for speedy loading and stacking at the port, as well as giving greater protection against damage and cutting down the losses through pilfering at the port of despatch or port of unloading.

The 1972 dispute originated in March 1971, when a T&GWU official argued that the employees at Midland Cold Storage in Hackney (not a container depot) should belong to the T&GWU instead of their present union, USDAW (Union of Shop Distributive and Allied Workers). There were only 57 employees at Midland, 28 in the cold store. By autumn Midland found that their trade had diminished and that goods being sent to them were being 'blacked' or impeded.

By 22 May 1972, picketing began outside Midland, organised by the joint shop steward's committee of dockers. In contrast to the determined solidarity of the dockers, the employers who used Midland took no concerted action, other than deciding to save money and avoid trouble by ceasing to send their goods to Midland. The company slipped from a profit of hundreds of pounds weekly to a loss of over £2,000 weekly. The picketing had been highly successful.

The pickets did not need to stop employees crossing the picket lines. They simply noted the number of the lorry, which could be done in good or bad weather, or through the window of a pub. Lorry drivers knew that their vehicles could be 'blacked' at other docks, though some went through picket lines where there were angry scenes.

This curtailment of business and financial loss to the company through unofficial picketing seemed to be a clear breach of the Industrial Relations Act. Midland sent a complaint to NIRC under Section 101 of the IR Act. On 7 July the Industrial Court made an order granting interim relief against seven named dockers to refrain from blacking the firm's premises. This had no effect. The pickets wanted the jobs inside the cold store to be done by dockers at dockers' rates. Instead of a £25 weekly worker job, it had to be a £50 weekly dockers' job. No special skill was needed for the work; the dockers were claiming work which used to be done in the dock areas. Their picket slogans were simple and to the point 'them out, us in'. It was the same successful slogan as was later used by General Amin to drive the Asians from Uganda.

Other picketing disputes, involving certain transport firms that traded in the docks area, were taking place over the same period as the Midland Cold Storage dispute. On 23 March Heaton's Transport went to the NIRC with an application for interim relief. The Court did not have to decide whether the complaint was justified or unjustified, but that a *prima facie* case existed. It decided that there was, and that an unfair industrial practice existed which prevented the loading and unloading of the complainant's vehicles. The Court directed the respondents, the T&GWU, who were not represented, 'to refrain ... from continuing to take such action'.

On 27 March, Heatons applied for writs against the union. In disobeying the court order, the union was in contempt of court. On 29 March the NIRC (Sir John Donaldson presiding) said that Mr Jack Jones, General Secretary of the T & GWU had written to the Court saying 'in accordance with the TUC advice the union will not be participating in the proceedings and will therefore not be in attendance ...'. Sir John viewed this reply in the context of a contempt of court, and 'almost without precedent'. As this was the first occasion an order of the Court had been disobeyed, a modest fine of £5,000 was imposed. He warned the union that there was no limit to fines for contempt of court, and that all assets were liable to come under an order for this purpose.

The T & GWU did not pay the fine, Heatons applied for a writ of sequestration, and the Court imposed a further fine of £50,000. The writs were issued on 21 April.

Another transport firm, Craddocks, brought a complaint to the NIRC on 11 April, alleging unfair industrial practice under Section 96 (1): 'It shall be an unfair industrial practice for any person, in contemplation or furtherance of an undustrial dispute, knowingly to induce or threaten to induce another person to break a contract ...'. The company wanted the order to help reach a negotiated settlement with the union.

The Court said that it was not its function to give either party weapons for bargaining. Its function was to act as a referee and declare a breach of the rules. There was a *prima facie* case and an interim order similar to that issued to Heatons was granted. The union again ignored the order, and on 17 April the Court, on Craddocks' motion, ordered the union to pay the costs of the motion.

By 20 April the NIRC was looking at the various cases of picketing continued in defiance of court orders. Sir John said that the fines had been small, but that the union had not sought to purge its contempt, and picketing had made it impossible for Heatons and Craddocks to carry their goods in the Liverpool and Mersey docks. The incidents were not to be treated as separate, but as continuing contempt of court, which could lead to sequestration of all the assets of the union. The Court had evidence that vehicles belonging to the complainants were to be blacked throughout the country. The union was directed to stop their 'officers, servants and agents' from acting in this manner. This had no effect as the container blacking dispute spread to London.

The Unions and the Courts

The heavy fines imposed on the T & GWU, and the shadow of further fines, led to a change of tactics on the part of the unions, though not all unions.

By 24 April the TUC had decided not to boycott the NIRC, and said that unions could defend themselves in court if necessary. This was not a change of policy, as they still opposed the IR Act, but it was necessary to allow unions to protect themselves and their funds. The million-strong Engineering Union disagreed with the TUC and voted not to appear before or recognise the NIRC.

The change in TUC tactics brought the T&GWU before the NIRC on 3 May, with an application to review the orders made above in the cases of Heatons and Craddocks. The judgement of the Court brought an explanation of its function. The rule of law must be upheld: 'if the rule of law is to have any meaning, the courts must in the last resort take action ... and impose some penalty'. (Heaton's Transport (St. Helens) Ltd. *v.* T&GWU). The NIRC was a court, but not a court of lawyers. There were members with experience of industrial relations, so that the judgement represented law and industrial experience. 'The Industrial Court is more than a court of law, it is a court of industrial common sense'.

Reviewing the case of Heatons, the Court said that the union had originated the blacking complained of and had not ordered its members to stop this. The union had written advising its members to obey the Court's orders; it had not said that industrial action must cease. Counsel for the union had argued that its policy was to decentralise power, and that the union could do little or nothing to stop the shop stewards taking industrial action. Removing them from office would make the situation worse. (In television interviews, dockers argued that removing shop stewards from office would simply lead to their replacement by other leaders who would function anonymously.) The Court said that the union was accountable for its members. Proper strikes were legal, but 'blacking' damaged employers, other workers and public. Those 'blacking' continued to get paid. The union must lead their members. The application was refused.

In mid May another firm, Analpina Services Ltd., applied to the NIRC for an interim order, complaining that its vehicles were being blacked at Hull docks. The T&GWU appeared as respondent. The order was granted.

The court orders were having no effect on the picketing, and shop stewards were giving press interviews. There was speculation as to which shop steward would be the first trade union martyr since Tolpuddle. One typical statement from a steward reminded of the possibility of fines or jail was: 'I will wait for the hand to come on my shoulder. We do not recognise this court'. (*Sunday Times*, 14 May 1972, p. 53).

The Court of Appeal

The container dispute and the widespread picketing, along with the NIRC's confirming that shop stewards were agents of the union, led the T&GWU to appeal against the contempt finding of the NIRC at the Court of Appeal. The fines had been paid, and the blacking was still taking place. If the union won the appeal, they would ask for the fines to be returned to them. Counsel for the union complained of the review judgement of the NIRC, and of their statement that blacking had been declared unlawful by Parliament, whereas it had not been so declared. The judges said that blacking was not unlawful if the union were registered. Mr Pain, for the union, argued that the strength of our law depended on what ordinary people like dock workers thought of it. He questioned the double standard involved in fining the union while the chairman of the stewards' committee responsible went unscathed while making statements defying the Court and its orders. Mr Pain said that at Hull, where one of the cases originated, a written agreement defined the shop steward's position, and he had no authority to take industrial action. The main point of the union's submission was that it had given sincere advice to the shop stewards who had not followed it, and they were only technically guilty.

Mr Yorke for the complainants argued that the shop steward relationship to the union was different from the master-servant relationship, and was something new to the courts, as quasi-servant or quasi-agent. The statement of the NIRC was recalled, in which the Court had said that lay members were always in a majority. The authority of shop stewards had not been decided by legal precepts, but by the industrial experience of laymen. One judge queried whether the NIRC took 'judicial notice of the facts of life' more than other courts, and was told: 'They don't sit in blinkers and they read the newspapers'. Another judge thought that the NIRC might say what material they used in reaching their conclusions. Mr Yorke complained that the rule book of the T&GWU was 'dreadful'. 'The Transport Union had handed over a vast amount of responsibility to the shop stewards and then disclaimed responsibility for them when something went wrong' (*TLR*, 6 June 1972). However, the Court of Appeal found for the union and held that shop stewards were 'acting outside the scope of their authority as agents of the union'. The Court found that the union was not liable for the action of the shop stewards in the case.

The Law and the Pickets

The refusal of the picketing workers to recognise or acknowledge the orders of the NIRC led eventually to collision with the law. This was not a confrontation between employer and worker, but arose from an application of the London (East) ICD Ltd. Manual Staff Association, representing T&

GWU members at Chobham Farm depot. They had been liable to dismissal if work were lost in the depot through picketing activities outside. The case was heard by the NIRC who said that the London Docks Joint Shop Stewards' Committee had picketed the depot, turning away lorry drivers and owners, with the aim of taking over the depot job for dockers. The Court compared the situation to a householder suddenly threatened by demolition by council employees. He would seek a court order restraining their action. The depot workers were in this position and were seeking the help of the law. The three dockers named had publicly disobeyed the order and continued picketing in a blaze of publicity. Warrants would be issued in two days time, so that the men concerned would have further time to cease picketing and explain their actions to the Court or appeal to the Court of Appeal.

This action was the first committal order made by the NIRC for disobedience of its orders. Sir John Donaldson said: 'By their conduct these men are saying that they are above the rule of law. No court should ignore such a challenge. To do so would imperil all law and order'. (*TLR*, 14 June 1972).

The drama was heightened as over 30,000 dockers went on unofficial strike and some other union leaders made militant declarations of possible strike action. Large numbers of pressmen and television crews assembled in the area to record the arrests for posterity. The press told the public that the Official Tipstaff, who was to make the arrests, was smaller in size than the militant dockers, and a prize fight atmosphere was built up. Anti-climax followed when, after some time, no officials appeared and news came that there would be no arrests. The scene was now pure comic opera, with some dockers playing a role that could have been from 'The Gondoliers' and saying 'we demand our wrongs'.

The official explanation for the late reprieve of the dockers was just as bizarre. The Official Solicitor, who was little known to the public, or indeed to the magistrates who deal with some 98 per cent of all court cases, appeared to represent the dockers concerned. Some difficulties arose as neither the dockers nor the union had asked to be represented. Legal custom requires that a barrister be briefed by a solicitor who is approached by a client. A barrister was prepared to appeal the committal orders as based on insufficient evidence. The difficulty was overcome by the Official Solicitor approaching the Court of Appeal and briefing the barrister, as he was entitled to do, on behalf of the dockers who refused to be defended. The Court of Appeal set aside the committal orders on the grounds that the evidence against the three dockers was insufficient. There was no proof that they had disobeyed the NIRC restraining order, or that they had not been picketing peacefully. (*TLR*, 16 June 1972). This case illustrates the difficulty of trying to settle an industrial dispute in court, and the stringent nature of legal evidence. The Judge and the laymen in the NIRC, with industrial experience, had been satisfied by the evidence. The Court of Appeal, with three judges, was not. We should note also that the three dockers would have been arrested for contempt of court, on the NIRC order, had it not been for the intervention on their behalf, but without their consent, of the Official Solicitor.

The reprieve had little effect on the scale of picketing outside the container depots by the dockers. Their attitude was that they did not recognise the Industrial Relations Act, nor the courts or bodies which interpreted it. The NIRC order to desist from picketing still stood, and events moved towards a further clash with the law. *The Times* was apprehensive, both about the possibility of a national dock strike and of the flaws in the Industrial Relations Act. It queried whether 'it is safe to have an act' which could precipitate 'a Grade A industrial crisis' on a private application for rights under the Act. It believed that the consent of the Attorney General should be obtained first, as the docks dispute was partly political and partly industrial.

As predicted, another interim order was granted on 7 July by the NIRC against seven dockers, who were allegedly picketing Midland Cold Storage depot. The order was intended to prevent threats of blacking goods vehicles entering or leaving the depot. The named dockers took no notice of the order, and the NIRC, which read the newspapers as part of its duty, must have noted that one picket was quoted as saying that the Court's judgements were 'of no more value than toilet paper' (*The Times*, 8 July 1972). Counsel for the men was briefed by the Official Solicitor. Counsel for the employers concerned asked the judge in Chancery for leave to serve notice of High Court proceedings. This was intended to reinforce the order from the NIRC restraining acts in tort. Permission to approach the High Court was given, but the dockers' leaders told the press: 'We will carry on doing what we think is right. This court will not dictate to us' (*The Times*, 8 July 1972).

The NIRC had considered the reversal of their judgement on the illegality of picketing by the Court of Appeal, under Lord Denning, who had ruled that peaceful picketing was lawful under Section 134 of the Act. The NIRC faced also the problem that evidence that it had found convincing had been insufficient for the Court of Appeal, though it agreed that it should take notice of the rulings of the other court. One difficulty was that the NIRC prided itself on its lay members and general industrial knowledge gained from press, radio and television. In this it had a wider knowledge of industrial relations than had the older and more formal type of court. An order was granted banning the dockers from blacking (Midland Cold Storage Ltd. *v.* Turner and Others).

Like the previous court orders, this had little effect on the picketing or blacking. This was affecting more firms than the public knew as some firms decided not to complain, which might have lead to further reprisals against them by the dockers. One letter to *The Times* from a docks employer said that there had been redundancy, but that the dockers were protected from the worst effects of redundancy by the highest redundancy payments granted to British workers. 'Voluntary severance' meant that a docker could receive up to £2,330. In spite of these arrangements, dockers were seeking the work done by other men, and saying to employers: 'Either you employ us or we will wreck your business and get rid of the workers that way' (*The Times*, 12 July 1972).

Some dockers were arrested and imprisoned for contempt of court. The resulting sequence of events deserve a page in legal history, for the 'Pentonville Five' became better known, though no less significant, than the Bettes-hanger Miners of 1941 who demonstrated that the rule of law in a democracy (even in wartime) broke down in the face of large scale defiance. Unofficial strikes broke out in the docks and other industries in support of the five dockers. The TUC called for a one day national strike on 31 July, and events were moving towards a major confrontation between the Government and the unions. MPs took up the debate. Conservatives insisted that the rule of law was on test, and that freedom and democracy rested on law and order. Left wing Labour MPs argued that the freedom of our citizens had been built on the workers' defiance of bad law throughout the centuries. Mr Wedgewood Benn recalled the spirit of the Tolpuddle Martyrs, and cast the Pentonville Five in the same mould as fighters for freedom. Mr Reg Prentice, Labour spokesman on industrial relations, thought that the Labour movement should not waste its sympathy on men who had so obviously and needlessly sought martyrdom. The official Labour position was that the Industrial Relations Act was bad law, but that even bad law should be obeyed and change sought through constitutional and parliamentary methods. The debate continued on television and radio and in the press. It was clear from the growing labour unrest that further imprisonment would lead to serious industrial trouble. Few insisted that the law should be enforced. The feeling appeared to be: 'A way will be found to get the men out of prison'. This had to be done without loss of face on the part of the Government and the NIRC, and the catalyst appeared in the shape of the ubiquitous Official Solicitor.

The three obvious difficulties in obtaining the release of the dockers were: (a) their gross contempt of the court; (b) their apparent unwillingness to purge this contempt by an apology; and (c) their refusal to be represented legally. The difficulties vanished like smoke before the wind when the House of Lords delivered a judgement in the case of Heatons. The judgement overturned the decision of the Court of Appeal, which had made shop stewards responsible for their own actions, and reaffirmed the original decision of the NIRC, holding that the unions were responsible for the actions of their shop stewards.

Within two or three hours of the House of Lords decision, the Official Solicitor was back in front of the NIRC, arguing that the dockers should be released as the employers could now proceed against the unions. The NIRC said that the men should be released, and Midland Cold Storage could pursue their action against the funds of the union concerned. Professor Griffiths has argued that the House of Lords decision holding that unions were responsible for the actions of shop stewards did not change the position of the five dockers. They were members of an unregistered union and this did not in law excuse them. 'The offence of the dockers for which they were imprisoned was not 'blacking' but defying an order of the court' (John Griffiths, 'Reflections on the rule of law' *New Statesman*, 24 November 1972). Griffiths' view is that the release of the five dockers was based more on political than on legal grounds.

The decision took the strength from the mounting wave of strikes, and the official union leadership took the initiative away from the militants. The T & GWU had been meeting with employers over several years to discuss the growing redundancies on the docks due to modernisation and container-isation. The results appeared in the Jones-Aldington Report, which brought considerable concessions to the dockers, more work guarantees and, severance payments of £4,000 for unfit dockers and those over 55 years. This alone put the dockers in a privileged position among manual workers. The Labour Opposition in Parliament pressed the point home by contrasting the peaceful negotiations of the Jones-Aldington Committee with the strikes and threats of strikes caused by the use of the Industrial Relations Act.

Most dockers felt that concessions had been wrung from the employers by militancy, and were still enraged by the imprisonment of the five shop stewards. The dockers delegate conference which met to consider the Jones-Aldington proposals voted against acceptance by 38 to 28, with 18 abstentions. There was much lobbying outside the meeting, which may have influenced the delegates. The issue was jobs more than money, as the number of men on the dockers' register had fallen by one third in seven years. With an ageing labour force and a tightly knit kinship system of fathers, sons and relatives, this made job security the key issue.

The failure of the proposals led to an official national dock strike beginning on 28 July. The Secretary of State for Employment was concerned that the proposals were rejected by 28 delegates from 84: he said little about using the emergency procedures of the Act, such as the cooling-off period and the ballot, though he was pressed for a secret ballot by Conservative backbenchers. The Opposition pointed out that it was the presence of the unregistered ports which irritated dockers from the registered ports. A few days earlier, in the debate on the events of 25 July, Mr Wilson said that the Industrial Relations Act 'was proving the most irrelevant and expensive legal bauble in history'. The Prime Minister retorted: 'The issue is whether these men are to be allowed to opt out of the rule of law'. Though some Labour MPs argued that the dockers were justified in defying bad laws, Mr Wilson and his main spokesmen said the law, even bad law, should be obeyed, though the Act itself should be repealed or suspended (*The Times*, 28 July 1972).

The national dock strike lasted some three weeks (28 July – 16 August) and had an adverse effect on some industries, as well as a delayed effect on the balance of payments. Picketing clashes occured at the unregistered ports on the east coast, as these continued to load and unload ships. Accusations were made about 'flying pickets' as busloads of dockers arrived from the main ports to picket the unregistered ports. The police eventually used road patrols to intercept groups of dockers and turn them back.

As in the case of the miners and the railwaymen, the Government footed the bill for an improved offer to the dockers. The agreement was to attempt to make all groupage container depots give jobs to workers at dockers' rates. This virtually doubled the wages of the semi-skilled workers who were stuffing and stripping containers outside the dock areas. Finally the Government agreed to pay the costs of the new redundancy payments of up to £4,000 per man.

The House of Lords decision (Heaton's Transport and others v. T&GWU)

The important ruling which enabled the five dockers to be freed was delivered on 26 July, when five law lords of the House of Lords heard the case of Heaton's Transport, Craddock Brothers, Panalpina Services and Panalpina Northern. The dispute between the transport firms and the T&GWU had been pursued since February-March 1972. Containerisation had resulted in less men employed at the docks; further loss of jobs was feared. The union was asking that stuffing and stripping containers for sea transport should be work reserved for dockers. It was union policy to pursue this aim by industrial action.

The action began in Liverpool with the Merseyside Joint Committee of Dock Workers and Road Traffic Workers (the 'Joint Committee') made up of shop stewards and not set up by union rules. It was 'unofficial' but acknowledged by the T&GWU, whose officials attended its meetings. The Joint Committee drew up an agreement and sent it to employers in the area. This asked for union recognition and an undertaking that the companies would not stuff and strip containers. Another Liverpool circular, presumably from the Joint Committee, demanded an overstamped trade union card as a condition of admission to the docks.

Heaton's application to the NIRC in March for an injunction against the union to stop blacking eventually led to a fine of £5,000 on 29 March and £50,000 on 20 April. This led to changes in TUC policy and the T & GWU finally appeared before the NIRC.

The T & GWU defence was that the general secretary had written after each injunction to the regional secretary. The latter had written to the shop stewards and advised them against industrial action. The same procedure was followed by the union in Hull as in Liverpool. Panalpina's vehicles had been blacked in Hull. The NIRC had refused the application of the T & GWU against the fines and orders. The Court of Appeal allowed the union appeal, saying that shop stewards had exceeded their authority as agents, and the union was not liable.

The House of Lords reviewed the background of the case. As the union was not registered it was liable to be cited for 'unfair industrial practices' under Section 96 of the Act. In citing this, the House of Lords criticised the Court of Appeal, who had overlooked the distinction between registered and non-registered unions. The unregistered T & GWU was to be dealt with as an organisation of workers. The law lords agreed that there had been blacking; that it had been organised by the shop stewards and court orders had been defied; that this was an unfair industrial practice under Section 96 of the Act. The question was, which party was liable in law? The union, as the normally responsible body, or the shop stewards organising the blacking? The case turned on the Court of Appeal view that the shop stewards were agents rather than servants. The law lords thought it better to ask whether the servant or agent was acting for, or in the authority conferred by, the master or principal. The relevant section of the Act, Section 167(9) says:

> Any reference in this Act to a person taking any action within the scope of his authority on behalf of an organisation shall be construed as a reference to his taking that action in his capacity as an official or agent of the organisation in circumstances where he is authorised, by or under the rules of the organisation or by virtue of an office in the organisation which he holds or otherwise, to take that action on its behalf.

The House of Lords found that shop stewards in the T & GWU, in rules and practice, had been given an implied authority to act for their members, by negotiation or by other action. Union policy was to retain container work. Shop stewards on the docks had organised blacking of haulage firms and the NIRC had found the union responsible. The union should have done more than write to the shop stewards telling them to stop industrial action: they could have relieved them of their authority as shop stewards, or taken disciplinary action. The law lords agreed that the union was responsible for the actions of its shop stewards in the blacking complained of.

Aftermath of the Dock Strike

The TUC reaction was to circulate a report to its affiliated organisations, in which the implications of the judgement were discussed. As most rule books gave some authority to shop stewards, this should be looked at carefully, although the alternatives of forbidding shop stewards to take industrial action without Executive permission, and of expelling shop stewards, would expose such stewards to liability in law. Unions should issue advice on noncooperation and on avoiding legal liability. The position of unregistered unions in blacking activities was now very uncertain and their funds were liable to proceedings from injured parties.

Experts on industrial relations pointed out the future difficulties created by the judgement. The T & GWU had never, in the last twenty five years, exercised any effective control or authority over militant dockers or unofficial dockers' leaders. If removed from their positions as shop stewards, the same men, or others, would appear as unofficial leaders. The closed shop was illegal, so the union could not remove the men from their jobs by disciplinary action. The judgement could lead to a large unregistered but official trade union, and a 'splinter group' of militant dockers who would carry all dockers with them.

The settlement of the dock strike and the large concessions on redundancy and jobs arising from the Jones-Aldington Committee did not stop the blacking activities, which continued as before. The difference was that the aggrieved companies decided not to use the law, as it was counter-productive. The militants were dissatisfied with the official settlement, as they wanted no redundancy, all unregistered ports to be brought into the dock labour scheme, and all container groupage to be done by dockers, distance from the ports notwithstanding. Mr Jones succeeded in the abolition of the unattached register and a pledge of no redundancy, but only a promise to look at the non-registered ports ,and 'a firm guarantee of 290 jobs' in container depots in the next year could be given against the dockers' other demands. Some of the companies who had been blacked were unwilling to agree to the last point.

The dockers' conference voted to end the strike and accept the proposals by 53 votes to 30. There were rowdy scenes outside Transport House, where the militants were massed in force, when the result was known. The delegates who voted against acceptance declared themselves to the crowd. Those who had voted against had to run a gauntlet of jibes, kicks and punches. Mr Jack Jones announced that disciplinary action would be taken against those responsible, but six months later the union's disciplinary sanctions appeared to be even less effective than those of the Industrial Relations Act.

Picketing continued at Midland Cold Storage (who were criticised by the dockers as being part of the large and rich Vestey organisation which had prospered in the docks) and some road haulage firms. By mid October a 'partial agreement' to lift blacking had been reached with one or two firms while others were still making approaches to the Industrial Court. In mid October Midland announced the sacking of twenty seven men due to the picketing activities, and the loss of £80,000 for the same reason. The T&GWU had made clear that the picketing was unauthorised, but this had little effect. A T&GWU shop steward at the depot said: 'We have tried everything to get the picket off the gate but have failed. It is incredible that the men are losing their jobs because of others from the same union' (*Financial Times*, 14 October 1972). By late November lorry drivers were threatening to break through the picket lines, but feared that their lorries would be blacked. In November the NIRC announced that 'no official of an organisation will be sent to prison for contempt of court'. The penalty would be financial. (*The Times*, 13 November 1972.) This was a recognition of the strong feelings roused by imprisonment, which had worsened industrial relations. Unofficial leaders of strikes were also unlikely to be sent to prison for contempt. There was also a recognition by the Government that the Act was only being used by a few small employers or individual workmen. Many companies simply avoided the picket lines by trading elsewhere, as they did not want their lorries blacked or their goods delayed for weeks.

Like the miners and the railwaymen before them, the dockers scored a resounding success by a combination of unofficial militancy and official negotiation. The Jones-Aldington Report was of enormous benefit to the dockers, as it doubled their redundancy pay from £2,000 to £4,000. But is is unlikely that negotiations would have succeeded without the picketing and pressure of the militant dockers.

As with the miners and railwaymen, the Government announced a settlement cost which was much lower than the eventual cost later. The docks scheme was to cost £9 million but cost over £30 million. This was due to serious underestimates of the number of men who would apply for severance pay and leave the industry. The estimate was 1,500; the figure was nearer 7,500. As many dockers had served for twenty five years they received the maximum of £4,000. The irony was that the fit men took the money and went to work elsewhere, while the unfit men clung to the job (*The Times*, 29 January 1973).

Legally, the effect of the differences of opinion between the NIRC, the Court of Appeal and the House of Lords showed the weakness of legal argument in settling disputes in industrial relations. The House of Lords decision that shop stewards were agents of the union and that their union was responsible for its agents, may be arguable at law but is demonstrably removed from the facts of dock life. Shop stewards are elected by the men and responsible to them; in the docks the first loyalty is to the dockers' cause, only secondly to that of the union.

The curious case of the five dockers led Lord Devlin to question the passing of laws which were not based on consensus. He argued that the courts have a neutral role in politics and their high status must not be used to support decisions which seem to the minority to be Government decisions. He gave the example of Part VIII of the Industrial Relations Act, where the Court granted the Secretary of State a compulsory ballot in the railway strike and a cooling-off order. His main point was the need for consensus law and 'the Industrial Relations Act is not based on consensus' (Lord Devlin, 'Politics and the law' *The Sunday Times*, 6 August 1972). This conclusion raises the whole point of the rights of the minority, when the majority of the voting public are in favour of the law.

The AUEW and the NIRC

It had become clear by the end of 1972 that nearly all major employers had decided to avoid using the Act, but this could still be triggered off by a small firm. In the case of the picketing on the docks, it appeared that small firms had also found the Act counter-productive and had ceased to use the NIRC. This left the unhappy worker as the new spark in the powder keg. The next clash between the NIRC and a major union came through the application of Mr Goad, an AUEW member, that he had been unreasonably excluded from meetings of his union branch. The union branch case for refusing Mr Goad entrance to their meetings was: that he had joined and left the AUEW three times; that he had worked during a one day unofficial strike in his factory, and refused to give his day's earnings to charity. He had also been a member of the T & GWU.

Mr Goad took his case to an industrial tribunal under the Industrial Relations Act, Section 65, which states that no member shall be debarred from attending union meetings by 'arbitrary or unreasonable discrimination'. The case before the Tribunal showed that Mr Goad applied to join on 8 October 1971, received a card on 11 October, and was warned away from the branch on 24 October 1971. It is arguable that Mr Goad could have been refused entry to the union on the grounds of his erratic union membership, but he had been given a union card and this, to the Tribunal, meant acceptance by the union. The AUEW did not appear before the Tribunal, as it is more fiercely opposed to the Act than most other unions, and had criticised the T & GWU for appearing before the NIRC. The branch continued to exclude Mr Goad, and he applied to the NIRC under Section 65. The AUEW did not appear, and was fined £5,000 for contempt of court on 8 November 1972. The union refused to pay and an order was made that the money be sequestrated, plus £1,000 for the costs of collection. The second appearance before the NIRC was on 8 December 1972. The union again refused to attend court and Sir John Donaldson commented: 'The problem in the union's eyes was not Mr Goad but the Industrial Relations Act... the union... has deliberately challenged the authority of this court and the right of Parliament to pass a law of which it disapproves' (Goad v. AUEW, *TLR*, 8 December 1972). The Court imposed a fine of £50,000 in addition to the original £5,000.

The union objected to the original fine and to their bank for having paid it. An action before the NIRC established that a writ of sequestration against assets in a client's account must be paid. (Eckman and Others v. Midland Bank Ltd. and Another, *TLR*, 7 December 1972). The union leaders said they would not pay the second fine voluntarily, that they would explain to their members the case of Mr Goad, and that they expected their members to support the policy of the union.

The action moved to the VAC factory where Mr Goad was employed as a quality control inspector. The men there refused to work with him, and he was sent home on full pay. The union branch still refused to obey the NIRC order. Mr Goad told the Press that he would abandon his attempt to join the union if the company gave him a 'golden handshake' of £30,000. His estimate was based on his calculated earnings plus bonus and pension for the next twelve years, after which he would be of retirement age. This statement was greeted angrily in trade union circles. Mr Scanlon, interviewed on television, said that the NIRC was a politically motivated court, and was opposed by his union for that reason. 'I don't think our members will sit idly by, and allow our union to be ruined.' He contrasted the speedy action by the Court over the Goad case, with the two or three years his injured members had to wait for compensation cases. The law might say that men are free to join a union, but unions must be free to apply their rules.

Mr Goad declared: 'It is the law of the land. My stand has strengthened the law'. In fact, the Goad case weakened the Act even further. There were a number of strikes in different industries, one in the VAC factory where Mr Goad worked, on this issue. Though not as many as the union had anticipated, there were sufficient to mark the degree of militancy caused by the Goad case. The union issued a twenty-four hour strike call to 350,000 engineering workers, and Fleet Street unions joined in. Months after the

NIRC ruling, Mr Goad was still excluded from his union branch, although he announced that he had temporarily ceased to try to enter.

There was public discussion over the nature of democracy. Why, some asked, did Mr Scanlon speak of the democratic wishes of his members, when a relatively small percentage of them had voted for his election as President of the AUEW? In contrast, the Government whose laws he refused to recognise was elected on a vote in which over 70 per cent of the electorate participated. Opinion polls had shown that over 70 per cent of voters favoured the main principles of the Industrial Relations Act. The union answer was that fundamental legislation of this kind needed lengthy discussion and negotiation with the unions; this had not taken place and the legislation had been forced through Parliament by the guillotine process on a small majority. But the Goad case provided yet another example of the 'crumbling' of the eight pillars of Mr Carr's Act.

The TUC and the Act

In the first year of the Act, many MPs and some industrial commentators forecast that union resistance to registration and to the main principles of the Act would wither away and that there would be a gradual acceptance of the will of Parliament. This did not happen, possibly because of the large scale confrontations between the Government and the miners, railwaymen and dockers, and the arrest and imprisonment of the five dockers which led the TUC to call a one-day national strike. In this atmosphere of confrontation between unions and Government, there was little chance of the moderate and white collar unions breaking away from the militant unions, as had been predicted, and registering under the Act.

At the 1972 Trades Union Congress the AUEW proposed that Congress continued with the policy of non-registration and co-operation with the Act. Any union which registered should be expelled or suspended from the TUC under rule 13. If any union were brought before the courts, they should be supported by all means including industrial action. Mr Scanlon told Congress: 'The courts under the act are brazenly political and do not appear to operate under the ordinary rules applying to other courts.... We believe that the general council has departed from Congress policy by advising unions to attend the industrial court' (*The Times*, 7 September 1972). He did not advocate a policy of total non co-operation with all the institutions of the Act, which was TUC policy, as he said that industrial tribunals, which predated the Act, could be used.

Other speakers called for a total boycott of the Act and all its works, as the surest way to bury the Act and lead to its repeal. They argued that the history of the labour movement had shown that united action could defeat 'reactionary lawyers'. The opposition to the left wing call for 100 per cent boycott and militancy against the Act came from the more moderate and white collar unions, such as the clerical and postal workers. The UPW argued that a total boycott would leave the unions defenceless in court, and the postal workers intended to appear when attacked and defend themselves. The ASTMS said defence was necessary, and that some 3,000 workers had appealed to tribunals on unfair dismissals. The unions could not abandon such people. Mr Feather urged the rejection of the left wing motion of total opposition, though the Act had worked demonstrably badly throughout 1972, as in the nonsense of the rail ballot which cost £150,000 to find out that the railwaymen supported their leaders ('we told him that for nowt'). The AUEW motion of total non co-operation was defeated by 2,198,000 votes.

One motion by the NUBE (Bank Employees) called on Congress to use the parts of the Act 'which it is in the interests of their members to so do'. The motion was not called, as the 90,000 NUBE members, along with thirty four other unions, were suspended from membership. Those suspended included the Confederation of Health Service Employees, the National Graphical Association and the British Airline Pilots Association (BALPA). At one time it seemed as though some of the large unions such as the Steelworkers, the Electricians and the Shopworkers (USDAW) might remain on the register, but the events and militancy surrounding the five dockers in July and August saw them joining the solid ranks of the TUC opposition.

Some of the suspended unions, such as the Seamen (NUS) and the Actors (Equity) had registered as the only method by which they could retain the closed shop necessary for their survival as unions. Without the closed shop Equity would not have a minimum wage or an effective organisation, as it had to face three federations of large employers, 'countless ephemeral fly-by-nights' and had many unemployed members. BALPA said that its members flew the world from Australia to Zambia. Nearly all countries had legislation similar to the Industrial Relations Act, and unions seemed to flourish in spite of this. Registration was necessary for BALPA, which felt that it was only the threat of suspension or expulsion which stopped many other unions from registering and using the Act. The number of members of the suspended unions came to half a million, and the TUC could not afford continued blood letting of this nature.

TUC hopes for the future were based on the Labour Party winning the next General Election and fulfilling their pledge to repeal the Industrial Relations Act. The Labour Party was officially committed to the repeal, although views differed on the legality of the unions' resistance and whether the law should be obeyed or resisted, but the official spokesmen had little sympathy for the martyred dockers. They also implied that there was no point in paying out union funds in court fines, or in political strikes against the Act, which should be changed by constitutional means. The Labour Party leadership was well aware that a national confrontation in 1973 between the Government and a major union or unions over pay, and leading to strikes or legal action, could result in a General Election fought on the rule of law, with the odds on 'law and order' as an electoral slogan.

8 The Courts and Tribunals

The work of the NIRC

The NIRC was set up as a labour court, of the type which exists in many democratic countries in Western Europe and in North America. The Ministry of Labour, in evidence to the Donovan Commission, was cool towards the proposal. It admitted that there were arguments for labour courts of 'ease of access, quickness, informality and cheapness', along with the chance for employers and trade unionists to sit in judgement, along with lawyers, and bring to bear a specialist knowledge of industrial relations, which ordinary courts did not possess; but it was unhappy at the prospect of laws in industrial relations being enforced by the courts. Donovan suggested that the existing industrial tribunals be enlarged and renamed labour tribunals. They should consider 'all disputes between the individual worker and his employer'. This would be an improvement on the variety of courts and tribunals which existed before 1970, with a tribunal hearing a plea for redundancy pay and the county court hearing a plea on unfair dismissal. The negotiation of collective agreements should be left to collective bargaining, but 'the decisions of the tribunal should be enforceable like those of a county court. An appeal should lie on a point of law to the Queen's Bench Division of the High Court'. (Donovan Report, p. 159). The TUC agreed with these suggestions, but did not want the tribunals to cover disputes which would 'involve interpretation of collective contracts.' It wanted to avoid references to 'labour courts' and wanted the tribunals named 'employment tribunals'.

The Court and the Act

The judgements of the NIRC, its differences of opinion and interpretation with the Court of Appeal, and the vindication by the House of Lords of the NIRC's judgement that unions were liable for the actions of their shop stewards, have been described earlier. The NIRC's clashes over the issue of the picketing dockers, and its decisions in the case of the Secretary of State for Employment *v*. ASLEF, received a great deal of publicity and comment. The failures of the NIRC have received far more attention than any successes or partial successes which it may have had in interpreting the Act. If we look at the way in which issues have arisen under the various sections of the Act, we may see judgements emerging that are having some effect on industrial relations.

The NIRC has nine lay members, and the intention was that employers nominees would be balanced by trade unionists. The trade union boycott led to a panel drawn from the employers, either working employers or from an employers' association, two retired business executives and two academics. The unions argue that the court is political and employer dominated, but it does have more industrial experience than any comparable court of law. This experience, and the professed informality of the court, is seen as an advantage by the layman, but seen with suspicion by the High Courts. It is for this reason that differences of opinion arose between the NIRC and the Court of Appeal on some important points, such as peaceful picketing and the nature of evidence.

The Court then, was conceived in adversity, denounced as employer-dominated and politically reactionary. The trade union movement refuses to co-operate with it, though most will now appear before it to defend themselves. The great majority of employers have no intention of bringing unions to court for issues arising from industrial relations, and none of the large employers have done so. Under these circumstances, it would be easy to dismiss the NIRC as a total failure, the 'most expensive legal bauble in history'. While the Act itself has been largely a failure, and the influence of the NIRC minimal, at times disastrous, the Court has had some effect on the shaping of industrial relations. This we shall now consider.

The NIRC, in the case of Heatons Transport *v.* T & GWU, described itself as 'a court of law, but not of lawyers', 'a court of industrial common sense'. We shall look at the NIRC from the viewpoint of an industrial relations specialist, to try to estimate how far it has applied 'common sense' to industrial relations.

The independence of the Court from political, industrial or governmental pressures has been stated by its President. Nor does the Court follow the Act in pedantic detail, as the intention is to interpret the guiding principles of achieving good industrial relations through collective bargaining, considering community interests, the freedom and security of the individual worker. Parliament set out the framework of industrial relations rules, within which 'strong and responsible' trade unions and employers can negotiate in an orderly manner. We have already noted that such phrases conceal more than they explain, and can be best understood from the judgements of the Court. For example, the above does not mean a 'free-for-all' with the strong winning at the expense of the consumer and community; and 'trade union' means 're-gistered trade union' as the advantages and protection of the Act do not apply to unregistered unions. The distinction is important, as the House of Lords pointed out in the Heaton case, in considering which it said the Court of Appeal had overlooked this.

The Act gives workers the right to be a member 'of such trade union as he may choose'. This includes the right 'to take part in the activities of the trade union', and, conversely, the right not to be a member. It is an unfair industrial practice for the employer to hinder this activity. The TUC feared that this section of the Act might lead to 'splinter' or breakaway unions, weakening the existing unions.

The NIRC faced this section in the case of The Post Office v. Ravyts (1972). There were appeals by the Post Office and the Union of Post Office Workers (UPW) against the decisions of some tribunals giving members of the Tele-communications Staff Association (TSA) the right to carry on trade union activities on the employer's premises. The NIRC overturned the decisions of the Tribunals, holding that even members of a registered union, such as the TSA, did not have the right to carry on trade union activities against the wishes of the employer. Discrimination against an individual worker demanding his rights as a member of a registered union was wrong, but the employer could discriminate against the registered union itself.

The dispute arose as the TSA, which had 10,000 members, was not recognised by the Post Office for negotiating purposes. The Post Office negotiated with the UPW, which had over 200,000 members, of whom 26,000 were telephonists. The UPW appeared before the NIRC, as did the Post Office. Fifteen cases of discrimination by the Post Office were alleged by the TSA, most of them arising from the Post Office's denial of union facilities which had been granted to the UPW. The NIRC found discrimination on two of the fifteen complaints; that the TSA member should be accompanied by a TSA official if he wished, when he was involved in a grievance or disciplinary matter; that private letters should be delivered to TSA members in the Post Office, as they are to UPW members.

The NIRC declared itself neutral on the issue of which union the employer should recognise, counting this a matter on which the employer should decide according to how he judged the industrial relations position. At no point does the NIRC appear to have considered the obvious point, that the Post Office did not want a number of small unions, any of which could disrupt the postal and telecommunication services, and preferred to negotiate with the large UPW. From any industrial relations point of view, this was the best position for the Post Office to take, and the NIRC recognised the facts of life in this case and reaffirmed its judgement in the case of King v. the Post Office, but said also that an official of a registered union does not have a statutory right to an interview with his employer. The case was brought by the same union, the TSA.

Other bodies besides the Court of Appeal disagreed with the strict inter-pretation of the Industrial Relations Act. The Industrial Arbitration Board judged an appeal in July 1972 by the AUEW, that Multiplex Designs Ltd., which did some government work, was in breach of the Fair Wages Resolution 1946, by saying that there was insufficient evidence of any breach. The important comment of the Board was that 'trade union' could also mean unregistered unions, and it suggested that companies doing contractual work for the government might give full rights for employees to join unregistered trade unions.

The NIRC took a different view of the status of an unregistered trade union in the case of Kenyon v. Miller, where Mr Kenyon, a worker of some two months standing, sued for unfair dismissal and said he was dismissed for taking part in union activities. Under Section 5(1) of the Act he could sue, if a member of a registered trade union. A tribunal had already ruled that this was the reason for his dismissal, but as he was a member of the AUEW, which had de-registered before Mr Kenyon's dismissal, he had no right to sue. The NIRC. agreed with the Tribunal's decision and ruled that 'trade union' meant 'registered trade union'. This ruling was strictly correct in terms of the Act, but it seems unrealistic to rule that as some 90 per cent of the trade unionists of Britain are in unregistered unions, they have no rights against being dismissed for union activities. As another tribunal ruling pointed out, the 'right to be a member of a trade union under Section 5 (1a) means only registered unions'.

The position of agency shops or union shops under the Act was dealt with by the Court of Appeal in the case of Hill v. C. A. Parsons & Co., Ltd. The plaintiff had not been a union member before 1968. After that date the Draughtsmen's and Allied Technicians' Association (DATA) had organised most of the firm and gained exclusive negotiating rights. By May 1970, after a strike, the company agreed to see that their employees would be required to join DATA within twelve months. The plaintiff had not joined the union and, after an initial warning, the firm gave him one month's notice ending on 31 August. The firm said they were honouring their agreement with the union. The Court of Appeal ruled that one month's notice was too short for a professional man of the plaintiff's standing; that his notice of dismissal should not terminate his employment, which should continue until Part II of the Act gave him the right not to join a union, in which case his employers could not dismiss him without laying themselves open to a charge of unfair dismissal; this was 'a clear case' for an injunction to be issued.

The Court of Appeal did not say what the appropriate length of notice was for a man with thirty five years service, earning £3,000 yearly, and with two years to serve before retirement, but the extension of the date to include the case before the Court (ending mid November 1971) brought the judgement to a convenient verdict. The Contracts of Employment Act 1963 was revised in 1971, with changes coming into effect on 28 February, 1972. The right to notice of an employee with fifteen years service is a minimum of eight weeks. It may well have convinced other unions and employers not to bring union shop (100 per cent membership) cases before the courts, which ruled in the above case that, as DATA was unregistered, it could not make an 'agency-shop' or 'approved closed-shop' agreement.

An agency shop agreement was reached with the cinema managers employed by EMI Cinemas. This was preceded by a ballot organised by the CIR under Section 12 of the Act which states that if a majority of those voting, or two thirds of those who do vote, wish an agency shop, then an agreement must be made by the employer. This was the first agency shop ballot carried out by the CIR, which gave the result to the NIRC at the end of October 1972. There was no need for a hearing in court.

Although the closed shop as such is virtually prohibited in the Act, Section 17 allows an application to be made where the union or unions, and employer or employers want an approved closed shop agreement; the application is usually examined by the CIR, who have to satisfy themselves that the closed shop will assist in the organisation of workers, achieve and maintain reasonable terms, conditions and stability of employment, stabilise collective bargaining and prevent the frustration of collective bargaining. Successful applications were made by the Seamen's Union (NUS) and Equity (for the acting profession).

One section of the Act contains an important new right for the worker, that of protection against unfair dismissal. Many of the unfair dismissal cases have been heard by the industrial tribunals, which have also dealt with redundancy cases in the past. Cases of unfair dismissal have been increasing, as more than 1,000 cases had been referred to tribunals between 28 February 1972 and the end of July 1972. Such cases are usually handled first by the Department of Employment conciliation officers. The Department dealt with 2,932 complaints of unfair dismissal, from which the above 1,000 cases were referred to tribunals. Of the latter, 27 per cent of the 500 complaints heard were successful. Opposition and trade union criticism focused on the 73 per cent of cases that failed. Samples of cases taken in November and December 1972 showed the number of successful claims to be rising, with December having just over 30 per cent.

The tribunals can recommend re-engagement, but this was only done in six cases in the first five months of operation. The amount awarded in compensation by the tribunals showed this to be higher than the amount reached by voluntary agreement. Though only 7 per cent were awarded between £1,000 and £4,000, 8 per cent got between £500 and £1,000, 49 per cent between £100 and £500, and 36 per cent received less than £100. In one case where the employee refused re-engagement, his compensation was reduced by some 15 per cent. Conciliation led to the re-engagement of 15 per cent of the cases settled.

The main work of the NIRC in connection with unfair dismissal cases lay in appeals against the decisions of tribunals. Some of the tribunal decisions were overturned by the higher court; for example, an offer of 'alternative employment' made by an employer must be specific. In turn, as we have seen, the judgements given by the NIRC can be taken to the Court of Appeal, as was done in the case of Brindle *v.* H. W. Smith (Cabinets) Ltd., where the Tribunal awarded £3,000 compensation to Miss Brindle, and the NIRC allowed an appeal by the company against the decision. The Court of Appeal allowed the appeal against the NIRC judgement and sent the case back to the NIRC.

An important ruling of the NIRC has been in laying down the principles for the assessment of compensation. This was in response to an appeal against a tribunal. The Tribunal had awarded the man in question four weeks' wages at £25.60 weekly plus compensation for the abrupt dismissal after 11 years service. It had awarded a total of £250. The NIRC ruled that the man should receive six weeks, wages, not four, as he was entitled to six weeks notice, plus £20 for unfair dismissal, plus £200 for loss of redundancy (or half his estimated redundancy pay at the time of his dismissal). This brought the total figure to £375.

Although the trade unions have denounced the Industrial Relations Act and all its works, it is NIRC judgements such as the above that are having an influence on union negotiations with employers. We have already noted that voluntary redundancy settlements were lower than those reached by tribunals. We now find that the NIRC has set still higher figures. These will now act as a yardstick for future redundancy settlements between workman, union and employer.

Other judgements relating to redundancy stated that the closure of a business after a group of men had refused to accept a new contract did not mean 'self-induced redundancy'; that an employee is redundant unless he is offered alternative work of a suitable kind; that the refusal of work (a one-day strike) was not a repudiation of a contract. These judgements have been seized on eagerly by union negotiators, as have been the guidelines for dismissal and disciplinary procedures, mentioned in the Code of Practice, that have been supported by a number of tribunal and NIRC. judgements. The guidelines mention oral warnings and written warnings of misconduct, with no dismissal for a first breach of discipline. Written statements on disciplinary action should be given to the employee and to his representative. Employer criticisms have to be passed on to the employee, and his contract of employment should embrace his specified work or duties. As few firms have such detailed dismissal and disciplinary procedures, the Code of Practice, buttressed by legal decisions, is now helping to change and build procedures in industrial relations.

The recognition of the NIRC as fulfilling the functions of a labour court was stated by the Chancery Division of the High Court in February 1972. Mr Justice Megarry said that Parliament intended that cases relating to industrial disputes should be handled by the NIRC. He said this in rejecting an application for an order stopping dockers outside Midland Cold Storage from blacking the depot.

The concept of 'unfair industrial practice' arises under the Act. This can apply either to action by the employer against workers or unions, or unions against employers or workers. Union rules and procedures can come under the scrutiny of the Court or tribunals if the member appeals against the action of the union; for example, one Tribunal said that disciplinary action should not have been taken by a union against a member who volunteered for redundancy (Forrest v. National Union of Sheet Metal Workers, 15 August 1972). The disciplinary procedure of the union was criticised, on the same lines as criticism had been made of the disciplinary procedures of employers. On the other hand, a tribunal held that refusal to work with a non-unionist was not an unfair industrial practice, nor was it a closed shop.

The NIRC, in another case relating to an appeal by ASTMS against an employer allegedly discriminating in contravention of Section 5 of the Act, said that a complaint by an employee was 'between himself and the employer'. It was not necessary for the union to appear in the proceedings. This decision fails to grasp the role of the union in representing employees when it is necessary to interpret an agreement (Mucci v. Imperial College of Science and Technology, 30 November 1972). ASTMS appeared in another NIRC judgement, where it had given one week's notice of a strike. This was insufficient, and the NIRC suggested an interval of fourteen days. This was a recognition dispute, where four men had been dismissed; a further complication was the fact that the employer was a travel agency and the union had plans for its own travel service (Horizon Holidays Ltd. v. ASTMS, December 1972).

Section 33 (4) of the Act refers to 'irregular industrial action short of a strike', intended to further an industrial dispute 'with the intention of preventing, reducing or otherwise interfering with the production of goods or the provision of services', and which is a breach of contract or service. 'Unfair industrial practices' are referred to and defined in different sections of the Act, such as Section 154 which mentions the enforcement of court orders against offending organisations.

The House of Lords dealt with the blacking dispute in Heatons v. T & GWU, and the NIRC and the Court of Appeal with 'irregular industrial action short of a strike' in Secretary of State for Employment v. ASLEF, two of the great legal set pieces of the industrial scene in 1972. The House of Lords ruled that the T & GWU was not a 'trade union' under the Act, as it was unregistered, but it was an organisation of workers, so complaints could be made against it. The complaints alleged blacking, that this had been organised by shop stewards, that such action was an unfair industrial practice. But the central complaint was one of authority. Could the shop stewards take action on behalf of the union? The judgement was that the union was responsible, through its shop stewards, for an unfair industrial practice.

This judgement had little effect on the practice of industrial relations. The blacking continued, and was modified through negotiation, as would have happened had the Act not existed.

'Irregular industrial action' and breach of contract were the central issues in the rail dispute, and lead to the 'emergency procedures' in Part VIII of the Act. The case raised a whole host of related issues: 'go-slow', 'work-to-rule', 'withdrawal of co-operation' and 'overtime ban'. The NIRC held that refusal to work on Sundays was not a breach of contract, nor was the refusal to work on rostered rest days. The union had told the men to book off after eight hours duty. This was held to be a breach of contract, as was the case of the signalmen who would not stay in their box until the last train had gone. The NIRC and the Court of Appeal both agreed on this, and also that the work-to-rule was unreasonable. Both agreed that the intention of the rule book was to help run the railways in an efficient and safe manner. The work-to-rule was intended to frustrate this objective.

The lawyers representing the rail unions argued that there was no legal rule which said that a man should do a fair day's work, and that efficient working was due to goodwill by the employees. It was not a breach of contract if they withdrew their goodwill.

The Court of Appeal held that men were paid for services rendered, not for producing chaos by deliberate acts.

This judgement was legally correct, but there are many ways which workers can use to frustrate the production of goods and services. In the USA, the police are forbidden to strike, but they have mass 'go-sicks' and 'go-quicks', where they book motorists for every small infringement, to put pressure on local politicians.

The NIRC was faced with claims for separate recognition by small and highly qualified groups of engineers and technologists. If pursued by a large number of such groups, this could lead to fragmentation of collective bargaining. An important case was that of the United Kingdom Association of Professional Engineers and others (UKAPE) *v.* Rolls Royce Associates Ltd. and others, in July 1972. Rolls Royce recognised three white collar unions: ASTMS, the Association of Professional Executive and Computer Staff (APEX), and the AUEW Technical and Supervisory Section (AUEW-TASS).

UAKPE claimed that it represented the most highly skilled and qualified of the white collar group, and that the above unions catered for a larger, less skilled membership. UKAPE claimed that the larger unions bargained on behalf of the less skilled groups, and that the highly skilled workers suffered by comparison; it asked the NIRC for a reference to the CIR, so that an investigation could be made. The Court was concerned that the numbers concerned were some 1 per cent. This was not enough in itself to refuse separate standing as a bargaining unit, providing the group concerned was a homogeneous unit with interests different to other employees. The engineers claimed that they made a special contribution to the prosperity of Rolls Royce, but the Court found no evidence that they were able to function effectively as a separate bargaining unit, or that a CIR investigation should be held.

UKAPE also appeared before the NIRC in April 1972 (UKAPE *v.* AUEW-TASS) alleging that the AUEW-TASS discriminated against UKAPE members by refusing to work with them or handle their work. The allegation was that this constituted 'irregular industrial action short of a strike' and could be called 'blacking on the job'. But the dispute arose from the struggle between ASTMS and DATA to organise white collar workers, that was eventually settled by negotiation and the award of sole negotiating rights to DATA for employees at a certain level in the firm of C. A. Parsons. (The effect of Section 5 (2) of the Industrial Relations Act on this agreement was referred to in the case of Hill *v.* C. A. Parsons & Co., Ltd.). A later development was that AUEW-TASS and ASTMS should together represent the higher technical staff and TASS the lower. Some of the higher technical staff, numbering 174, wished to be represented by UKAPE. The matter had been referred to the CIR on 29 February 1972 for consideration of the question of bargaining units for technical staff. The irregular industrial action complained of would hinder the inquiry, and was also a breach of the employees' contract. An interim order stopping the industrial action was granted.

The issue of bargaining units was also being settled without reference to the NIRC or the CIR. A recognition agreement between the National Union of Bank Employees (NUBE) and a building society was dealt with by the Department of Employment conciliation procedure. The ballot was carried out by the Electoral Reform Society. The NUBE was successful in obtaining recognition from a number of building societies.

The NIRC held private meetings and awarded sole bargaining rights to the EEPTU (Electrical Engineering Staff Association) in the firm of British Relay Ltd. Two legally enforceable agreements for five years were concluded. Other private meetings of this nature, illustrating the conciliation aspect of the NIRC, were held in late 1972. In 1972 the Court dealt with some fifty cases of bargaining rights. Although the Act was interpreted against some 'splinter' professional associations, it gave recognition to some groups, such as the Commercial Union Group Staff Association, after the CIR had reported and asked that the Association should become financially independdent of the Company by raising its subscriptions. This was done, though it raised the argument as to which unions were 'independent' of employer control, and which were not.

We have already dealt with the issues of emergency procedures in the case of the railways dispute and strike. This brought Mr Macmillan before the NIRC to obtain (a) a 'cooling-off' period, and (b) a ballot of union members in the dispute. He asked for twenty one days 'cooling-off' and was given fourteen days. The ballot was carried out by the CIR and was, as predicted, overwhelmingly for the union action and against the Railways Board's pay offer. The railway unions won a substantial pay increase; the Government's incomes policy was breached yet again, and the emergency procedures of the Act were discredited. They were not used again in 1972, nor were they revived in the sporadic strikes of early 1973, when the gas workers and the hospital workers could clearly 'endanger the lives of a substantial number of people' or cause 'serious risk of disease' or 'personal injury' under Section 138 (2)(b) of the Act. It is ironical to consider that the normally peaceful gas workers, forbidden to breach contracts of service by striking under Section 4 of the Conspiracy and Protection of Property Act 1875, had the 1875 Act revoked under the 1971 Industrial Relations Act (Section 133) and went on unofficial and official strikes in February 1973.

The Act also failed to control picketing by unions. This activity was allowed under certain conditions and forbidden under others, such as pursuing an illegal strike, inducing a breach of contract, and infringing workers' rights. The Court of Appeal judgement referred to above, that peaceful picketing is not an unfair industrial practice, was rejected by the NIRC. These legal judgements failed to stop the picketing at the docks and depots by dockers, and had no effect on the August 1972 strike and picketing by building workers. In the case of the miners' and building workers' strikes, there were widespread complaints of 'flying pickets' – squads of militant workers who were transported from one picket area to another to strengthen the picket lines. Some of the pickets did not belong to the union in dispute. The question of the secondary boycott, or action by strikers to persuade others, not in their industry or dispute, to breach their contract, was shown vividly during the miners' strike of 1972. The important question is not the illegality of many forms of picketing during the above strikes, but whether the law can be enforced. In the case of the miners, the Government ignored the breaches, as did the police. In the builders' strike the Act was not invoked, although the police took more action in controlling picket lines and violence. Some pickets were fined for breaches of the criminal or civil law, but it seems likely that the strikers 'passed the hat round' to help pay their fines. It appears that future picketing disputes are more likely to be left to the judgement of the police on the spot than to any attempt at invoking the Industrial Relations Act.

The effect of the Act on collective bargaining has been due more to the joint negotiations of employers and unions than to 'placing industrial relations in a legal framework'. The great majority of companies decided not to use the Act; this includes the nationalised industries and the Civil Service. The illegality of the closed shop has not prevented its existence, though this now exists through what the unions call '100 per cent membership', and employers encourage, though they may not coerce, employees to join unions. This is more in keeping with the Code of Industrial Relations than with the Act. A number of agreements now exist, beginning with the words 'nothing in this agreement shall be enforceable at law'.

Some agreements were signed on a legal basis, omitting the above clause, and stating that there should be no sympathy strikes during the life of the contract. The EEPTU is one union which has signed such agreements in return for a single staff union. Such agreements would have been signed had the NIRC never existed.

All in all, the NIRC has had less of an influence on industrial relations than was hoped (by the Government) or feared (by the trade unions) at the time. There has been no procession of trade unionists being fined or imprisoned, though two large unions have been fined for contempt of court. There has been no effective order made against strikes, and official strikes by unregistered unions have greatly increased during the first full year of the Act. Little has been heard of the enforceability of collective agreements, the closed shop or the agency shop. There has been no development of 'splinter' unionism, as the CIR has favoured the continuation of the stable, larger unit, though some previous 'company unions' have been allowed to register as bona-fide trade unions. The great set-piece cases of the dockers and the railwaymen produced the judgement that the union is liable for the acts of its shop stewards, which proved in practice to be virtually unenforceable in the docks, while the emergency procedures legislation on the railways did nothing to hinder, and much to advance, the national strike which took place.

The main impact of the NIRC has been on the question of appeals arising from industrial tribunals, especially in the area of unfair dismissal. Settlements for the redundant and the unfairly dismissed employee have been higher than those reached through voluntary negotiation, while the judgements given and the criteria developed have been of use to trade union officials and shop stewards in their negotiations in these areas. Sir John Donaldson possibly had this latter activity in his mind when he said, at the end of 1972, that the main work of the NIRC had been as a 'small debt court, for which there was a great need in the British legal system'.

The Commission on Industrial Relations

The Commission was set up under the Labour Government in 1969, and was changed to a statutory body under the Industrial Relations Act in November 1971. Its object was to improve industrial relations according to 'the principle of collective bargaining freely conducted on behalf of workers and employers with due regard to the general interests of the community'. Under the Act the CIR carries out inquiries relating to trade union recognition; sole bargaining agents; ballots under the national emergency procedures; and approved closed shop agreements.

An example of the last-mentioned relates to the closed shop agreement in shipping. CIR Report no. 30 recommended to the NIRC that the National Union of Seamen (NUS) and the British Shipping Federation should be permitted to agree an approved closed shop. This was to 'promote and maintain stable arrangements for collective bargaining relating to the seafarers'. The Report commented on the difficulties of union recruitment with many short-term seamen, and new employees should join before they sailed. Seamen had to accept strict discipline on board ship, and a closed community should not have the element of conflict in a union member/non-member situation. The closed shop would help recruitment, stabilise industrial relations and help the enforcement of agreements. A strong union was needed for the policing of agreements, and the acceptance of responsibility in the joint disciplinary procedures of the industry. If there were no approved closed shop some employers might sign non-union crews and this would lead to industrial conflict. An agency shop was considered and rejected, as it might encourage the non-member and small groups in ships. The NIRC approved the closed shop in shipping.

The CIR, in its pre-Industrial Relations Act days, had done some reports on union recognition and representation. These established criteria relating to job skills, qualifications, systems of payment and group preferences, which were later used by the CIR in its work under the Act (see R. Lewis and G. Latta, 'Bargaining Units and Bargaining Agents', *British Journal of Industrial Relations*, March 1972).

Bargaining rights were examined in the case of C. A. Parsons & Co., Ltd. (CIR Report no. 32). The Report was sent to the NIRC under Section 48 of the Act, and it said that there was a basic affinity in the functions of the technical staff up to, but not including, the assistant manager level. UKAPE claimed negotiating rights for a bargaining unit which could start from the level of new graduates entering the companies. The CIR rejected the UKAPE claim, and also that of the ASTMS, which would have created difficulties with salary structures, negotiations and work organisation. The recommendation was that the AUEW-TASS should be recognised as the sole bargaining agent.

116

The procedures for recognition under the Act may be set in motion by the Government, with an application to the NIRC by the Secretary of State for Employment, or by an application by a trade union or unions, or employer and union, or employer. The reference is passed to the CIR by the NIRC. The former carries out a survey and makes a recommendation. The agent named, or the employer, applies to the NIRC for the CIR to carry out a ballot. The NIRC then makes its order, if the majority voting is in favour of the bargaining agent.

Though the procedures for and definitions of the sole bargaining agent and bargaining unit are specified in Sections 44, 45–50 and 52–55, (withdrawal of recognition is under Section 51), this is also underlined in the Code of Practice under the heading 'Bargaining Units'. Factors include nature of work, training, experience, qualifications, common interests, employee wishes, working conditions and payment (Code of Practice, paras. 74–81, p. 18–19). These would seem to work in favour of the status quo, as the factors include 'the need to fit the bargaining unit into the pattern of union and management organisation' and 'avoid disruption of any existing bargaining arrangements which are working well'. The Code also points out that the first objective of employer and union should be to reach a voluntary agreement on the issue. Only after this fails should they move to conciliation through the Department of Employment and then to the CIR and the NIRC.

Two references will show the method of the CIR in recommending sole recognition to a union. The first reference is to the first report after the CIR became a statutory body. The reference on Engelhard Industries Ltd. (CIR Report no. 6) was first received on 16 November 1970, then re-referred on 4 November 1971 by the Secretary of State for Employment under Section 121(1) of the Act. The Report was made some two months later, in January 1972. It showed that 27 per cent of manual workers were union members and a further 51 per cent would join if the union were fully recognised. The recommendation was made for the AUEW.

The other reference also recommended full recognition and negotiating rights to the AUEW. The inquiry found that 75 per cent of all employees were 'actual or potential' AUEW members, and another 22 per cent were willing to join if recognition were granted. The objections of the management to the union are set out in some detail, as are the attitudes of the union. New procedures and institutions are suggested by the CIR, such as a strengthened works committee, grievance and bargaining procedures, and other aspects of industrial relations.

In these, and other reports, the CIR has worked towards the recognition of strong and responsible unions, the reform and wider scope of collective bargaining, and the need for a campaign to develop industrial relations policies as 'an integral part of the total strategy with which it pursues its business objectives' (CIR Report no. 34: 'The role of Management in Industrial Relations'). The last-mentioned report stressed the need for clear and written policies, wider knowledge of industrial relations amomg senior and middle management, and the recognition of labour relations as a major management function.

In addition to its surveys and reports on industrial relations in particular companies, the CIR has carried out important surveys on general topics mentioned in the Code of Practice and the Act. The Code mentions 'disclosure of information for collective bargaining' (IR Act, Section 158 (1)), and CIR Report no. 31 deals with the type of information that management should provide; for instance, manpower, pay, conditions, financial information, prospects and plans. While some of this information may be no more than that supplied to shareholders, and some may have to be treated as confidential, the legislation and the Report represent a considerable step forward in some industries.

The CIR's espousal of collective bargaining has surveys of wages councils in certain industries. Most wages councils had been set up because of the weakness of union organisation in the industries in question. Under the Wages Councils Act 1959, amended by the Industrial Relations Act 1971, the Secretary of State for Employment may refer such councils for abolition or a variation of their function. Fifteen wages councils were referred to the CIR in January 1972. An example of the CIR method of inquiry can be seen from the *Report on the Hotel and Catering Industry*, Part II: 'Industrial Catering', March 1972, which recommended the abolition of the Industrial and Staff Canteens Undertakings Wages Council. The grounds were that voluntary collective bargaining on pay and conditions covered 60 per cent of employees, and that 97 per cent of employees were being paid at or above the new statutory rate. Many rates were well above the statutory minimum. The employers thought the Wages Council almost totally irrelevant, while two of the three unions favoured abolition and the third thought abolition should be considered.

The work of the CIR is an extension of its role as a voluntary agency under the Labour Government, devoted to the improvement of collective bargaining. Its statutory tasks under the Act have been minimal, as there has been little request for the approved closed shop, agency shop, ballots, or recognition as sole bargaining agents. It has done important work in its surveys of companies and its suggestions for the improvement of collective bargaining and industrial relations. Its view of the need for far more industrial relations training is set out in Report no. 33, which, if supported and encouraged by the Government and other interested groups, would result in a far greater knowledge of industrial relations and a possible improvement in the conduct and climate of industry.

Discussion and education of this nature is less dramatic than contentious Parliamentary legislation on industrial relations, but it will produce more lasting results.

Industrial tribunals

The tribunals existed before the 1971 Act. They were created in the Industrial Training Act of 1963 to hear and judge appeals against levies imposed on employers by the industrial training boards. Their jurisdiction was extended under the Redundancy Payments Act 1965, where they dealt with employers and employees' rights under the Act. The tribunals also deal with questions arising from the Contracts of Employment Act 1963 (this task was given to the tribunals in 1965, and taken away from the civil and criminal law procedures). The tribunals spent most of their time before 1971 dealing with cases under the Redundancy Payments Act. They were supported by the trade unions in their work, and trade union nominees sat on the tribunals, as well as appearing before them to represent their members.

The Ministry of Labour referred to the tribunals as 'the nucleus of a system of labour courts' in its evidence to the Donovan Commission. The TUC, in its comments on Donovan, approved of extending the jurisdiction of existing tribunals 'to cover appeals against unfair dismissal'. This was done under the 1971 Act, which lists a number of new functions for the tribunals under two headings: (1) worker complaints about infringement of rights under the Act; (2) cases of unfair dismissal. The person presenting the complaint is the appellant, the other party the respondent. Forms of application are issued by the Central Office of Industrial Tribunals. The intention of the Act is that the tribunals deal with issues arising under workers' rights, although organisations and companies may have to reply to the complaints. The regulations apply to England and Wales; there are some small differences in the case of Scotland.

Before the 1971 Act the three-person tribunals contained one nominee from the unions, and one from the employers' panel. The TUC boycott led the Government to draw up one panel of people with relevant industrial experience, to flank the legal chairman. This has inevitably led to a marked drop in the number of people with trade union background or experience, and the average panel tends to be middle-class and employer dominated; the absence of union nominees changes the balance of opinion, and the panels are poorer for their absence.

It is interesting to compare the procedures of the magistrates' court with that of the industrial tribunal. It was the intention of Parliament that the tribunals should not be legalistic, but should try to promote good industrial relations. In fact, the tribunals are often more legalistic than the average magistrates' court. This arises from the composition of the tribunals. The chairman is a qualified barrister or solicitor of at least seven years' standing. He is usually a full-time chairman, and sits (in a regional tribunal) on every case, so that his experience and authority far outweighs that of the two laymen who flank him. As most of the decisions taken revolve round interpretations of the law, the industrial relations experience of the 'wingmen' is rarely used. By contrast, the magistrates' court is made up of two or three lay justices, advised on legal points by the clerk to the court. The justices decide most of the cases and the opinion of the legally qualified clerk is rarely needed. Justices appear to be less awed by legal arguments in court than are the laymen in the tribunals.

The legalism of the tribunals is enhanced by the growing trend for employers to be represented by a lawyer, while the TUC boycott means that most unions do not use the tribunals, and the individual workers who appear are rarely supported by union officials, as they once were. In these circumstances, the lawyer for the employer tends to direct his arguments at the tribunal chairman. While the latter might be mindful of the interests of the unrepresented appellant, the chairman cannot represent him. The result is that numbers of cases presented by appellants are badly prepared and poorly argued. Yet there is no legal aid available for persons or firms appearing before the tribunals. This puts the balance of advantage in favour of the employer.

In spite of the above disadvantages, legal and social, of the tribunals, the 1971 Act has opened a new area of workers' rights, particularly with regard to unfair dismissal. The tribunal is required to consider whether the employer was reasonable or unreasonable. Tribunals may adjudicate on actions for unfair dismissal (Section 22), also for a range of issues such as infringement of workers' rights as to trade union membership or activities (Section 5), actions over contributions arising from an agency shop agreement (Section 10), discrimination by organisations of workers against workers (Section 66), discriminations by organisations of employers against members (Section 70), and actions in breach of union rules by a trade union (Sections 81 and 107).

These represent the new juridictions of the tribunals, and cases have arisen relating to some of the sections outlined. But the main work of the tribunals relates to questions of redundancy, though the number of cases of unfair dismissal is increasing rapidly. There have also been well publicised cases of actions for infringement of workers' rights, either the right not to be a member of a trade union, or the right to join a trade union (for example, Goad v. AUEW).

Section 22 of the Act states that 'every employee shall have the right not to be unfairly dismissed'. An employer who does so has committed an unfair industrial practice. The employer must show that the reasons for dismissal relate to certain criteria. Compensation can be awarded if the employee is not re-engaged. The tribunal can recommend re-engagement but not reinstatement. Compensation is increased if the employer 'unreasonably refuses to re-engage'. It shall not exceed 104 weeks pay or £4,160, whichever is the less.

As noted above, the main work of the tribunals is with claims for redundancy, but claims for unfair dismissal have been growing. The reason for the changes illustrates the way in which circumstances alter legal cases. The first few years of redundancy payments saw large numbers of employees collecting, in some cases volunteering or requesting, redundancy pay related to their years of service. This was a once-and-for-all lump sum to many, as a man with twenty years service cannot collect another large sum for a considerable period. Large scale unemployment from 1970–72 also reduced the numbers who would voluntarily accept redundancy, while productivity bargaining, which had resulted in excess manpower being shed, became less popular due to unemployment. With the changing economic conditions, the unfair dismissal clause now represented an alternative or additional compensation to a displaced or dismissed employee. Instead of the arguments before the tribunal being (from 1965 to 1971) 'I was not dismissed, I was redundant', the arguments have been changing to 'I was not redundant, I was unfairly dismissed'. For this reason, many of the cases before the tribunals turn on the distinction between the two Acts, and require a greater knowledge of the industrial relations situations in the firms concerned.

The problems facing tribunals attempting to judge whether an employee who was dismissed was really redundant are not easy. For example, suppose an employer alleges inefficiency, or personal deficiencies, or bad personal relations, in order to dismiss an employee, how does the employee prove that the employer was attempting to avoid making a redundancy payment? An example of the way in which dismissal and redundancy can overlap may be seen from a case before a Manchester tribunal, where a man was dismissed for refusing to accept a combined job in a redundancy situation. The company said his dismissal was not unfair as they had applied the 'first-in, last-out' principle. The tribunal found no unfair dismissal, but said that this might apply in other redundancy situations. (Birtwistle v. Ward & Goldstone Ltd. ,1972, Incomes Data Service Brief, December 1972).

'Unfair dismissal' seems to be one section of the Act of which the trade unions approve. The judgements of the tribunals and the NIRC in this area give them a powerful bargaining lever in their negotiations with employers. As many of the cases are settled through the conciliation process of the Department of Employment, it seems that the conciliators are using the criteria developed by the tribunals and the Court, and are advising employers and employees what their chances of success would be if they decided to appeal. On the basis of conciliation and trade union negotiation, the great majority of cases are settled or withdrawn before reaching the tribunals.

Whatever happens to the Industrial Relations Act, there appears to be a future for the tribunals in their work on redundancy and unfair dismissal. This is rapidly establishing criteria of reasonableness and equity in the relationship between employer and workman. It also leads to the greater documentation and clarity of grievance procedures, and to the widening of the collective bargaining agreement.

There will also be a role for the tribunals under the Equal Pay Act 1970. The trade unions are sympathetic to the idea of equal pay, but have been slow, as have employers, in implementing the principle. Future cases may arise where women workers complain to the tribunals. Under the Race Relations Act 1968, a complaint may be made to the tribunal about discrimination in employment, though most cases are dealt with by Race Relations committees. The two areas of discrimination, one based on sex, and the other on colour, may lead to more cases in front of tribunals as people become more aware of the laws and the opportunities.

9 Wages and the Law

The belief that Britain is a country based on the principles of free enterprise, where rewards are related to the workings of the market economy, is a view that flourishes strongly only in the weeks before a General Election. The earlier economists wrote of 'the iron law of wages' which decreed that wages were a fixed part of the national income; their increase would lead to profits, and therefore investment, being diminished, and the national income would decline and people would be poorer. Though the theory was related to the economic dangers of the rapidly growing population of the Industrial Revolution, modern variants of the theory have appeared recently.

In any event, the Victorian belief in free enterprise and state neutrality towards industry and commerce had shown signs of distintegration by the early 1900s. By 1909, MPs. were insisting that firms which received Government contracts should observe a Fair Wages Clause (originally passed in 1891), paying wages comparable to good employers in the same industry and area. In the same year, the Trade Boards Act set up trade boards to advise on and regulate wages in certain 'sweated industries', which employed non-union labour in cramped back room premises. The intention of the Trade Boards legislation was to provide state support and inspection for workers (or employers) who were poorly organised and could be exploited. As union organisation improved, the boards might be dissolved. By 1946, the boards had become wages councils, and the present Wages Council Act dates from 1959. There are some fifty wages councils and, in the 1970s, they fix statutory minimum wages for over three million workers, mostly in the distributive, service and catering trades. Awards made by the wages councils have statutory force and must be notified by employers to their staff and carried out. Wages inspectors carry out checks to enforce the orders. Workers can sue for back pay up to a period of six years.

The modern approach to restraint on pay has appeared since 1945. The acceptance by the Conservative and Labour Parties of 'high' employment in one case and 'full' employment in the other has meant in practice that, together with demand inflation, prices have risen steadily since 1945, and quickly since 1968. Different economists have disagreed over the causal factors in inflation, but since the mid 1960s the general opinion has been that one of the main causes of inflation has been the fact that money wages have been increasing faster than the overall rise in productivity per head. Wages vary in their importance as a production cost, and it has been argued that as wage costs are some 40 per cent of all production costs, therefore they cannot be the main cause of inflation. Yet income from work accounts for seven eighths of all income, and the other eighth is income from property. While there are great differences in wealth and life styles in Britain, no large political party has come out squarely for equality of income, although the differences in income help to create political tensions which sometimes lead to industrial disputes.

In the mixed economy of Britain in the 1960s, the Labour Party won the 1964 Election on a programme for the planned growth of incomes. A prices and incomes policy was introduced with a Declaration of Intent, drawn up between the Government, pledging a high rate of employment and economic growth, the CBI, pledging employers to higher output and stable prices, and the TUC promising restraint in wage increases and co-operation in raising output. The policy had some effect in helping to raise output and interest workers in productivity bargaining, but frequent balance of trade and sterling crises led to a slow increase in economic growth and increases in direct and indirect taxation restricted the rise in workers' incomes. From 1964 to 1969 incomes from work rose by some 7 per cent per head per year as workers pushed for higher money wages to compensate for rising prices and higher taxation as their incomes rose and placed them in new, higher tax categories. By 1970 the rise in incomes from work was over 11 per cent and the 'wage explosion' was under way.

An analysis of national income figures shows that wage pressure had been squeezing profits as employers faced greater international competition, and were unable to act as they had done in the past and pass wage costs on to consumers in the form of higher prices. The share of profits in the national income fell while that of wages rose. The figures in Table 4 show the recent shift.

The falling rate of profit, and the relative failure of the incomes policy of the Labour Government, together with concern over rising prices, were among the factors which led the Labour Government to abandon attempts to

TABLE 4

	Income from employment (Percentage of total)	Income from self employment (Percentage)	Gross trading profits, surplus and rent (Percentage)
1968	68.0	8.1	23.9
1969	68.7	8.0	23.3
1970	70.3	7.7	21.9

Source: *National Income and Expenditure*, 1971

enforce statutory control of wages and turn to thoughts of a legal framework for industrial relations. The aim of this was to discourage the short unofficial strike or threat of it, which led to inflationary wage settlements. The legislation was withdrawn, but a more draconian legal framework was promised by the Conservatives during the 1970 General Election. One writer described the Labour Party Bill on industrial relations as 'a psychological substitute for an incomes policy'. The Conservatives introduced the Industrial Relations Act 1971 as a legal substitute for an incomes policy.

The Conservative Government recognised that no voluntary incomes policy could be arranged with the TUC in the prevailing economic and political climate of 1970–71. The Act was introduced as part of an election policy to put the unions in a legal framework and improve industrial relations. The Conservative Election Manifesto of 1970 also said: 'We utterly reject the philosophy of compulsory wage control'. Taxes would be cut, people would work harder, and prices would be cut 'at a stroke'.

The collapse of the Conservative policy of 'free' wages had been evident from the statistics. By November 1972, the index of earnings (allowing for seasonal adjustment) was rising by over 20 per cent over the previous year. Mr Heath admitted to the House of Commons in January that the earnings index was up 16½ per cent in November over the previous year, but argued that real incomes had increased by some 8 per cent, as the prices index had risen by 7½ per cent over the same period (*The Times*, 25 January 1973).

The argument over the various estimates of the price rise and the pay rise brought agreement on one central point: the British economy was suffering from acute inflation, which might escalate into a yearly rate of over 10 per cent. Pay claims in the pipeline in autumn 1972 showed a number of unions - miners, railwaymen, teachers, police, civil servants, electricity workers – all queuing to obtain 'substantial' pay increases which the Government feared would give another twist to the inflationary spiral. The British scope for economic flexibility, from devaluation to economic controls and restriction of imports, was also disappearing with entry into the Common Market in January 1973.

For these reasons the Conservative Government, which had made a number of ministerial speeches between 1970 and 1972 denouncing controls on pay or prices, or attempts at a statutory incomes policy, as folly, damaging to the leadership of unions, giving opportunities for militant shop stewards to ignore both leaders and the law, suddenly altered its policy and announced tripartite pay and price talks between the Government, CBI and TUC.

The rising tide of days lost through strikes showed the failure of the Industrial Relations Act 1971 to 'place the trade unions in a legal framework'. In 1970 the Conservative Manifesto had stated: 'in terms of the actual number of strikes our postwar record is among the worst in the world'. In 1972 the figures for days lost through strikes were some 24 million, over twice the 1970 figure of 11 million. The Government argued that 45 per cent of days lost was due to the coal miners' strike, and two thirds of all days lost resulted from the three great clashes with the miners, the dockers and the building trade workers. They pointed to the fall of 36 per cent in the number of work stoppages started between 1970 and 1972 as proof of the working of the Act.

The Act had some deterrent effect on the small unofficial strike; but it had been replaced by the large official strike, far more damaging to the economy in terms of days lost. As 90 per cent of all disputes were about wages, the Act had failed in its major objective of reducing the days lost through wage disputes. Whatever the legal apparatus of the Act, and the wide range of its many clauses, many influential people had expected the Act to curb inflationary pressures. For example: 'Two thirds of the directors who responded to a survey prepared on behalf of *The Times* expected that the Industrial Relations Act rather than a statutory incomes policy would reduce inflationary wage pressures'; and conversely: '55 per cent felt that a statutory incomes policy would not work'. (*The Times*, 13 February 1973).

The growing inflation and the threat of further strikes in the winter of 1972–73 made the Government change its mind on a pay and prices policy. But first they created the psychological climate for the introduction of a statutory policy by inviting the CBI and TUC to talks in 10 Downing Street in an attempt to agree a voluntary pay and prices policy.

Government economists calculated that £3,000 million could be available for extra earnings in the following year. This led the Government to offer the unions a ceiling of £2 weekly per worker, plus an average 60p allowance for 'wage drift' due to overtime and other earnings. Prices would be held at 5 per cent above the autumn 1972 figures. This meant that wages would rise by 9 per cent, earnings by 8 per cent, and workers would gain in real income by 3 per cent. The Government also promised to maintain a high rate of economic growth of around 5 per cent, nearly twice the figure of the 1960s, and to reduce the level of unemployment. Cost of living increases were to be paid on the basis of 20p for every point that the Retail Price Index rose over 6 per cent.

The CBI were in reluctant agreement with the ceiling on prices, as numbers of the large companies felt that they had made sacrifices under the CBI 'ceiling' of 1971–72, but they were prepared to accept the 'package' with its commitment to economic growth, higher production and higher profits.

The flat rate increase in incomes would have helped the lower paid and led to a levelling of the inequalities between social groups. The cost of living clause would have protected workers from the rise in retail prices. Some left wing economists were cordial towards the proposals, while suggesting a rise of £3.50 instead of the ceiling £2.60 per week.

The fundamental objections which came from the TUC dwelt on the inequalities of contemporary society, the large profits made by land speculators and agents selling houses and, the sharp rise in food prices. The Government had no effective control over prices and such controls should be introduced. It seemed to the TUC that pay was to be controlled while prices, and therefore profits, would float freely. It objected to the past rise in the cost of living, including the rises and future rise in council house rents. The Government should negotiate with the Common Market to reduce the rise in food prices. Lastly, the TUC argued that a 6 per cent growth rate would make possible a rise of £3.40 per week per worker, while a threshold clause in the cost of living index should be a payment of 30p for each 1 per cent over a 5 per cent increase. It also wanted the non-operation of the Industrial Relations Act.

After some weeks of talks, the proposals for a voluntary pay and prices policy were still unacceptable to the TUC, while the Government could not accept the TUC's counter proposals. At this stage the Government announced a 'pay freeze' on 6 November 1972. All increases in pay, prices, rents and dividends were to be frozen for ninety days. The standstill was to be reinforced by fines on summary conviction, not exceeding £400, and on conviction on indictment to a fine. The latter fine would be for defying a minister's powers under the Bill, and would not exceed £100. This was the second attempt at a pay freeze in seven years: the Labour Government had introduced a pay 'standstill' in mid 1966. Sanctions took the forms of fines up to £500. Enforcement proved difficult, but the pay 'freeze' succeeded for some months; this was due to general co-operation, not legal enforcement.

The Conservatives' dislike of statutory pay control was partly changed by inflation and the rise in strike-days. But another factor was the apparent success of the US pay-price policy of President Nixon. The US had reduced unemployment by 0.5 per cent, cut the rate of increase in the cost of living by half, and expanded production by 9 per cent through this policy. The Americans had begun with a ninety day standstill on prices and incomes, then set up a Pay Board and a Price Commission, with a tripartite structure of businessmen, trade unionists and public representatives, fifteen in all. Pay guidelines of 5.5 per cent increases were drawn up. The Price Commission settled on a 2.5 per cent average for price rises per year, and focused the attention and powers of enforcement mainly on the large firms. Legal sanctions were written into the legislation, but these were rarely used. The US Government had certain advantages in its pay-price policy which the British Government did not have: (a) this was the first attempt at such a policy for some twenty years; (b) food prices were relatively stable, while British prices were rising sharply for a number of reasons; (c) US unions sign contracts for two or three years, and the Government had seen some of the key unions sign shortly before the pay-price policy began; and (d) US unions influence only

127

25 per cent of the labour force, whereas the British unions influence over 40 per cent, and are politically more critical of the Government than the US unions. For these reasons alone it would seem that the British policy had less chance of success, although it had 70–80 per cent support in opinion polls.

The pay freeze was known as Phase I. Phase II was introduced on 17 January 1973 in a White Paper 'The programme for controlling inflation: the second phase' (Cmnd. 5205). The new Bill was to be enacted by 31 March, and the 'standstill' was to be extended by a further sixty days. Following the US example, there were to be two bodies, a Price Commission and a Pay Board. These would scrutinise and have powers over prices and profits. Manufactured goods could have limited price increases; profit margins would be limited, and large firms would need permission to raise prices. Food prices would be difficult to control and the Government hoped the price rise would be small. Increases scheduled for school meals and rents were to be postponed or scaled down. Rates would be subsidised further.

Workers were subject to pay controls. The White Paper stated: 'Pay is the largest single element entering into prices which are under our own control or influence', and they were an important factor in inflation as they had been 'running at 15–16 per cent above a year before'. Pay must come into line with the growth of output, and increases for groups of employees were not to exceed '£1 a week a head plus 4 per cent of the current pay bill for the group, exclusive of overtime'. This policy is on two tiers: the flat rate increase benefits the lower paid more in percentage and absolute terms, while the 4 per cent increase partly compensates the higher paid, although no individual is to receive an increase more than £250 a year.

Breaches of the policy, by 'striking or threatening to do so to force an employer to contravene a notice or order' amongst other offences, could lead to fines. Pay increases had to be notified in advance for firms of over 500 employees.

The TUC rejected the pay-price policy. The unions were already angry at the pay freeze, although the Government had been relieved to see the electricity workers and the police, key figures in industrial disputes, reach pay settlements before the deadline. The hospital workers, the civil servants, the teachers and the gasworkers, and other non-militant groups were caught by the standstill. The effect was to turn them into militants, threatening strikes, overtime bans and 'with-drawal of co-operation'.

The TUC supported the above in their actions. The Government were told, 'There can be no real and lasting answer to the inflation problem until the proposals of the Government and the unions come together'. The TUC proposals stated that a policy based mainly on wage restraint could not succeed. The Government's proposals, according to the TUC, would have meant that incomes from profits and dividends would rise one and a half times as fast as wages and salaries. The TUC wanted statutory controls on prices, mainly food, rents, housing, fares and fuel. Some foodstuffs could be subsidised; the tax concessions to the wealthy of the 1972 Budget should be reversed, and a wealth tax introduced; dividend restraint, taxes on land speculation, and other measures proposed added up to a £600 million cost to the Exchequer. The emphasis was on economic growth, which should rise to 6 per cent per annum, and more purchasing power in the economy would help achieve this aim. The proposals were in the TUC plan for countering inflation, 'Economic Policy and Collective Bargaining 19 February 1973).

The union proposals were buttressed by talks between the Labour Party and the TUC, reviving hopes of agreement on pay and prices between them for the first time in five years. The Labour Party programme was based on control of prices, not pay. Pay would be left to collective bargaining, with the lower paid in mind, and with the TUC adjudicating between rival union claims.

The sharp difference between Government and Opposition on the issue of combating inflation showed clearly the different social and political attitudes of the parties. There was an ironic reversal of roles since 1970; then, the Labour ministers were complaining of a flood of wage claims, and Mr Wilson was pointing out that 'one man's pay increase is another man's price increase' By mid 1970 the Conservatives, though complaining of price rises, were supporting an award to the doctors of 30 per cent. By early 1973 the positions were almost exactly reversed, although the taxation and social policies of the two parties were different.

Reaction to wage restraint

The national press was almost wholly in favour, and editorials were written telling the Government to stand firm against inflationary wage demands. The fact that the Newspaper Proprietors Association were in the habit of conceding to inflationary wage demands by the employees, and had found reasons for paying an award during the pay standstill, was noted sourly by Mr Grimond, MP. *The Times*, approving the pay-price policy as 'fair, workable and necessary', got to the nub of the question 'will it work?' by saying that 'it could only fail as a result of general and unlawful opposition by organised labour.... they have the power to bring the economy to a halt (*The Times* 18 February 1973).

Other newspapers pursued this theme and confidently predicted that if large scale strikes led to a confrontation between the unions and the Government over the issue of wages and inflation, the resulting election would be fought on the issue of 'Who runs the country, Government or unions?' and the Conservatives would win with a large majority. The Opposition argued that elections were fought on a variety of issues, and food prices and EEC entry, along with the Labour claim of an agreement with the unions on fighting inflation, would influence voters.

Union opposition to the pay standstill and the Phase II proposals mounted in early 1973. The gasworkers began with a number of unofficial industrial actions and followed with an official nationwide ban on overtime, coupled with selective strikes in certain areas. Hospital workers planned similar action from the end of February. Train drivers also banned unrostered overtime and rest day working and planned a one day national strike. Civil service unions, for the first time, considered a one day strike. Teachers in London took part in selective strikes and closed a number of schools. Ford workers voted to take part in a strike. The total number of workers taking part in industrial action by the end of February numbered three quarters of a million, while the miners and other groups considered joining such action in March.

One factor which may prevent the coming clash over Phase II is that legislation in March makes strike or industrial action illegal and union funds may be forfeit. Yet such legislation cannot be enforced against large numbers and it would be a hazardous move by the Government if they tried to seize union funds. These legal tactics have proved unsuccessful in countries such as Ireland, Australia and the United States, where union leaders have been imprisoned and refused to pay fines.

The important factor is the extent to which the country supports the Government's policy, and the recognition of this by union members, who represent a large section of the public. Legal action by the Government against groups of workers is not likely to succeed, as we saw in the case of the Pentonville five, where the dockers were improsined and quickly released when strikes broke out. Even if the law were to be strictly enforced, workers would find many ways of circumventing it, by go-slows, work-to-rule, overtime bans and withdrawal of co-operation.

Legal restraints on collective bargaining and wages can only be effective if the great majority of workers who are subject to the restraints are willing to accept them. This was the case in the USA during the pay-price policy of 1971–72, though this restraint was breaking down in 1973 as food prices rose sharply. A pay-price policy with legal enforcement can only work in Britain if the social consensus exists. This consensus can be created only if wage earners feel they are being treated fairly.

Unions and the Social Contract

It has been argued that the legislation on industrial relations introduced in

1971 was based on the need to contain wage-push inflation resulting from unstable and competitive collective bargaining. It was pointed out that earlier majority Conservative governments had made no change in the law during the years 1951–64, though there were signs of unrest over trade unions from some of their influential supporters.

The pay-price spiral of the late 1960s and early 1970s made some legislation inevitable. The point is that the legislation is virtually unenforceable; it is more complicated than the labour legislation of the USA, which was introduced over a period of some twenty years, while the British legislation was brought into law in twelve months. Furthermore, grievances in American industry are channelled through a system of arbitration, which is widely accepted, while British grievances explode into unofficial and official strikes (less in workdays lost than the US figure, but financially more damaging due to their unpredictability and the British trading position).

As some writers have said, union acceptance of an incomes policy is an acceptance of the existing social order. Unions exist to alter society, and an incomes policy, or legislation designed to put unions in a legal framework which severely restricts their collective bargaining, is likely to be resisted as the years 1970–73 have shown. Unions also fear that legislation on pay and industrial relations will not only impair their power to bargain collectively but may be designed to end the power of unions. Numbers of writers are forecasting that the trinity of stable prices, full employment and economic growth cannot be reconciled with free collective bargaining. Inflation is now becoming the major economic and social problem of the Western economies, just as unemployment was the major evil of the inter-war years, and future governments may agree with *The Times* of 18 February 1973, which said: 'It may well be true that unlimited collective bargaining ended in Britain on November 6th last year'.

It may be that there will be constraints from time to time on collective bargaining, as the government sees inflation rising over a given percentage figure, or there is a balance of trade deficit, or a currency crisis. But legal restraints on pay can only be effective if workers feel there is a sense of equity in the distribution of incomes. Policies of taxation, food and rent subsidies, more wide ranging social security and pensions, better systems of education, all help to create a fairer social system. In the field of pay, a Pay or Incomes Board might build up criteria which satisfy the sense of fairness that workers must feel in making comparisons between rewards in different jobs and occupations.

There is also a growing demand by workers to share in the decisions which influence their working lives. British industry lags far behind the eight other countries of the EEC in developing works councils and systems of worker directors. The EEC Commission made suggestions in late 1972 advocating an expansion of worker representation at board level. There are signs that the Conservative Government may move in this direction; the Labour Opposition are committed to the development of industrial democracy, while the Liberals have supported the statutory introduction of works councils for some years. The TUC are now more cordial to the idea of worker participation in industry, and seem prepared to develop the EEC proposals in this area.

There are no magic remedies for better industrial relations, nor is there any reason why industrial conflict cannot be accepted in a Western type mixed economy, where disagreements exist over the division of the product and the nature of society. But changes should be made in the system of industrial relations that can command the assent of unions and workers. The best chance of achieving a social consensus is by collective bargaining and negotiation, not by legal orders and sanctions.

Much depends on the nature of future governments, and the lessons they draw from the period 1969–73, when new forms of law were brought into industrial relations. A future Labour government is officially committed to the repeal of the Industrial Relations Act, and would move in the direction of the social consensus needed by the unions; but some legislation would still be necessary: unions argue that a development of the TUC machinery for resolving disputes, and a voluntary conciliation and arbitration machinery, could supplement normal collective bargaining. This still leaves the problem of unofficial action by powerful or strategic groups in such industries as docks, cars, airlines and other areas where swift industrial action, or the threat of it, can bring an inflationary settlement which triggers off a round of comparative wage disputes. Unions need to face up to this problem more than they have done so far, or even a Labour government will legislate on industrial relations as has been done in some Western countries by Social Democratic governments, such as those of the Scandinavians.

The present Conservative Government, or a future one, would have to recognise that the 1971 Act needs revision. We have shown that it is largely inoperative over much of the legislation. The unions do not recognise it, and employers avoid using it. The first change needed is on the question of registration: unions which have existed for eighty or a hundred years do not cease to be unions simply because a refusal to register makes them 'organisations of workers'. Unions should be registered on a voluntary basis as before, and the clauses should be dropped from the Act, along with the changes which this makes in the Act.

The whole question of emergency procedures needs to be examined. A 'national emergency', if the clause is retained, should be debated and sanctioned by Parliament, not by the NIRC, as the decision is primarily a political one. Some form of political 'filter' is also needed so that a national dispute cannot be triggered off by an application to the NIRC from an individual or an employer. Holland insists that action of this kind has to be screened by the government.

The closed shop legislation also needs to be changed. This should be allowed as an agreement between unions and employers. The right not to join should be dropped from the Act, and the issue left to voluntary negotiation or conciliation.

The NIRC may or may not survive under a Labour government, but the Tribunals could play a new important role in industrial relations, particularly in the area of unfair dismissal, where they could create a new and necessary protection for millions of workers.

Whatever form the revision of labour law may take, the changes need to be talked through on a tripartite basis between unions, employers and the government. Labour law, like other forms of law, must rest on a democratic consensus.

Bibliography

Historical

(Some of the material has been cited in the text, but this list will take the reader further into the subject).

Citrine, N.A. *Trade Union Law*, Stevens, London 1960 (3rd ed. 1967).

Hedges, R. Y., and Winterbottom, A. *Legal History of Trade Unionism*, Longmans, London 1930.

Phelps Brown, E. H. *The Growth of British Industrial Relations*, Macmillan, London 1959.

Pelling, H. *A History of British Trade Unionism*, Penguin, Harmondsworth 1963.

Webb, S. and B. *History of Trade Unionism*, Longmans, 1920.

General

HMSO *Royal Commission on Trade Unions and Employers' Associations*, (The Donovan Report), London, June 1968, (Cmnd. 3623).

Research Papers published by the Donovan Commission:

(1) W. E. J. McCarthy, 'The Role of Shop Stewards';

(2) A. Marsh, 'Pt. I Disputes Procedures';

(3) Marsh, A. and McCarthy, W. E. J., Disputes Procedures'.

Harvey, R. J. *Industrial Relations*, Butterworths, London 1971.

Jackson, R. M. *Enforcing the Law*, Penguin, Harmondsworth 1973, (revised); see Chapter 9.

Kahn-Freund, O. *Labour and the Law*, Stevens, London 1972.

Wedderburn, K. W. *The Worker and the Law*, Penguin, Harmondsworth 1965 (2nd ed. 1971) (also has an excellent bibliography);
Cases and Materials on Labour Law, Cambridge University Press, 1967.

Wedderburn, K. W. and Davies, P. L. *Employment Grievances and Disputes Procedures in Britain*, University of California, 1969.

Industrial relations

Balfour, C. *Incomes Policy and the Public Sector*, Routledge and Kegan Paul, London 1972.

Clegg, H. A. *The System of Industrial Relations in Great Britain*, Blackwell, Oxford 1970;
  How to Run an Incomes Policy, Heineman, London 1972.
Glyn and Sutcliffe *British Capitalism, Workers and the Profits Squeeze*, Penguin, Harmondsworth 1972.
Hughes, J. and Moore, R. *A Special Case?*, Penguin, Harmondsworth 1972.
Jenkins, P. *The Battle of Downing Street*, C. Knight, London 1970.
Knowles, K. G. J. C. *Strikes*, Blackwell, Oxford 1952.
McCarthy, W. E. J. *The Closed Shop in Britain*, Blackwell, Oxford 1964;
  'The Nature of Britain's Strike Problem', *BJIR*, July 1970.
McCarthy, W. E. J. (ed.) *Trade Unions*, Penguin, Harmondsworth 1972.
Runciman, W. G. *Relative Deprivation and Social Justice*, Penguin, Harmondsworth 1972.
Roberts, B. C. *Industrial Relations*, Methuen, London 1968 (revised);
  'Fair Deal at Work – A Review', *BJIR*, November 1968.
Turner, H. A., Clack, G., and Roberts, G. *Labour Relations in the Motor Industry*, Allen and Unwin, London 1967.
Turner, H. A. *Is Britain Really Strike Prone?*, Cambridge University Press, 1969.
Turner, H. A., Jackson, D. and Wilkinson, F. *Do Trade Unions Cause Inflation?*, Cambridge University Press, 1972.
Flanders, A. *Management and Unions*, Faber & Faber, London 1969.

Comparative Labour Law

Aaron, B. (ed.) *Labour Courts and Grievance Settlements in Western Europe*, University of California, 1971.
Gregory, C. O. *Labor and the Law*, W. W. Norton, New York 1961.
Kahn-Freund, O. *Labour Relations and the Law*, Stevens, London 1965.

Index

Compiler's note: Throughout this index the Industrial Relations Act (1971) is referred to by the initials IR Act

138

Date Due